Aberaeron	27	Llanstephan	36
Aberporth	35	Milford Haven	15
Aberystwyth	7	Narberth	30
Ammanford	9	Newcastle Emlyn	31
Brynamman	27	Newport	31
Cardigan	19	New Quay	32
Carmarthen	11	Neyland	32
Cross Hands & Cefneithin	20	Pembroke	23
Drefach	28	Pembroke Dock	17
Ferryside	35	Pen-y-Groes & Saron	25
Fishguard & Goodwick	21	Pontyberem	24
Glanaman & Garnant	22	St.Clears	33
Haverfordwest	13	St. David's	33
Kilgetty	36	St. Florence	37
Lampeter	28	Saundersfoot	34
Laugharne	36	Tenby	26
Llandeilo	29	Tregaron	37
Llandovery	29	Tumble	34
Llandybie	30	Whitland	35

Key to street plans
Allwedd i blaniau stryd

Plans drawn at a scale of 4 inches to 1 mile
Aruluniwyd y planiau yn ôl y raddfa 4 modfedd i 1 filltir

═M4═	Motorway	Trafffordd
A48	A road (Trunk road)	Ffordd A (Priffordd)
A48	Dual carriageway	Ffordd ddeuol
B4281	B road	Ffordd B
	Through road	Ffordd drwodd
- - - - - -	Track/Footpath	Llwybr/Llwybr troed
-··-··-··-	County boundary	Ffin sirol
-··-··-··-	Municipal boundary	Ffin fwrdeisiol
▬▬▬	Railway	Rheilffordd
▓▓▓	Woods and forest	Coedtir a choedwig

P	Car parks (major)	(prif) Maes parcio
✝☪	Places of worship	Mannau addoliad
🏠	Hotel/Public house	Gwesty/Tafarndy
	Petrol station	Gorsaf betrol
	Police station	Gorsaf heddlu
⊠	Post Office	Swyddfa'r Post
M ◼	Theatre/Museum	Theatr/Amgueddfa
T	Toilet facility	Cyfleustra toiled
✚	Health centre	Canolfan iechyd
	Caravan site	Safleoedd carafannau

Street plans prepared and published by Streetwise Town Plans Ltd., 3 Rayleigh Road, Basingstoke, Hampshire and based upon the Ordnance Survey maps with the sanction of the Controller of H.M. Stationery Office. Crown Copyright reserved.
©Streetwise Town Plans Ltd. 1995.

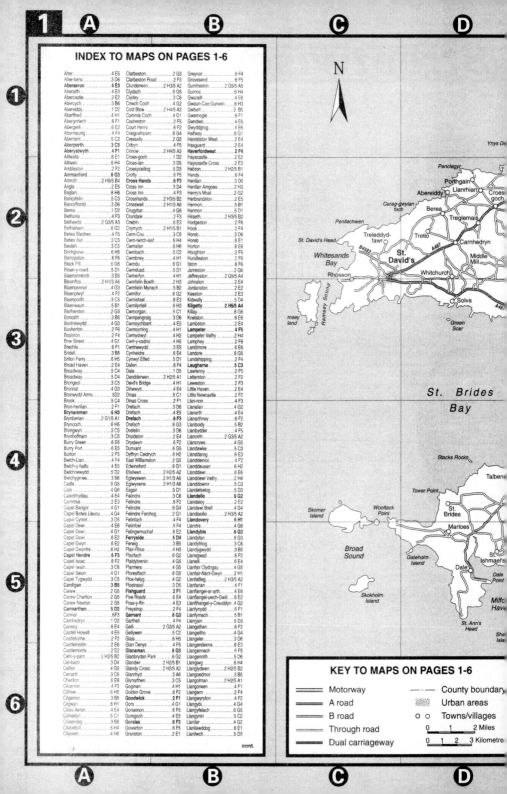

INDEX TO MAPS ON PAGES 1-6

Aber..............4 E5
Aber-banc..........3 D6
Aberaeron........**4 E3**
Aberarth............4 E3
Abercastle..........3 E2
Abercych............3 B6
Abereiddy............1 D2
Aberffrwd............4 H1
Abergorlech..........6 F1
Abergwili............6 E2
Abermeurig..........4 F4
Abernant............5 C2
Aberporth........**3 C5**
Aberystwyth......**4 F1**
Alltwalis............6 E1
Alltwen............6 H4
Ambleston............2 F2
Ammanford........**6 G3**
Amroth............2 H5/5 B4
Angle............2 E5
Baglan............6 H6
Bancyfelin..........5 C3
Bancyffordd..........3 D6
Berea............1 D2
Bethania............4 F3
Bethesda......2 G3/5 A3
Bethlehem..........6 G2
Betws Bledrws........4 F5
Betws Ifan..........3 C6
Beulah............3 C5
Birchgrove..........6 H5
Bishopston..........6 F6
Black Pill............6 G6
Blaen-y-coed........5 D1
Blaenannerch........3 B5
Blaenllos......2 H1/3 A6
Blaenpennal..........4 G3
Blaenplwyf..........4 F2
Blaenporth..........3 C5
Blaenwaun..........5 B1
Bletherston..........2 G3
Boncath............3 B6
Bontnewydd..........4 G3
Bosherton..........2 F6
Boulston............2 F4
Bow Street..........4 G1
Brechfa............6 F1
Bridell............3 B6
Britton Ferry........6 H5
Broad Haven........2 E4
Broadway............6 C4
Broadway............5 D4
Brongest............3 C5
Bronnant............4 G3
Bronwydd Arms......5D2
Brook............5 C4
Bryn-henllan........2 F1
Brynamman........**6 H3**
Brynberian......2 G1/5 A1
Bryncoch............6 H5
Bryngwyn............3 C5
Brynhoffnant........6 E6
Burry Green........6 E5
Burry Port..........6 F5
Burton............2 F5
Bwlch-Llan..........4 F4
Bwlch-y-fadfa........4 E5
Bwlchnewydd........5 D2
Bwlchygroes........3 B6
Cadle............6 G5
Caio............4 G6
Caledrhydiau........4 E4
Camrose............2 E3
Capel Bangor........4 G1
Capel Betws Lleucu....4 G4
Capel Cynon..........3 D5
Capel Dewi..........2 G5
Capel Dewi..........4 G1
Capel Dewi..........6 E2
Capel Gwyn..........6 E2
Capel Gwynfe........6 H2
Capel Hendre......**6 F3**
Capel Isaac..........6 F2
Capel Iwan..........3 C6
Capel Seion..........4 G1
Capel Tygwydd......3 C5
Cardigan........**3 B5**
Carew............2 G5
Carew Cheriton......2 G5
Carew Newton......2 G5
Carmarthen......**5 D2**
Carmel............6F3
Carnhedryn..........1 D2
Carway............6 E4
Castell Howell......4 E5
Castlebythe..........2 F2
Castlemartin........2 E6
Castlemorris........2 E2
Cefn-y-pant....2 H2/5 B2
Cei-bach............3 D4
Cellan............4 G5
Cenarth............3 C6
Charlton............6 E6
Cilcennin............4 F3
Cilfrew............6 H5
Cilgerran............3 B6
Cilgwyn............6 H1
Ciliau Aeron........4 E4
Cilrhedyn............5 C1
Cilwendeg............3 B6
Cilybebyll............6 H4
Cilycwm............4 H6

Clarbeston..........2 G3
Clarbeston Road......2 F3
Clunderwen......2 H3/5 A2
Clydach............6 G5
Clydey............3 C6
Cnwch Coch..........4 G2
Cold Blow......2 H4/5 A3
Commis Coch........4 G1
Cosheston..........2 F5
Court Henry........6 F2
Craig-cefn-parc......6 G4
Cresselly............2 G5
Cribyn............4 F5
Crinow........2 H4/5 A3
Croes-goch..........1 D2
Croes-lan..........3 D5
Croesyceiliog......5 D3
Crofty............6 F5
Croes Hands......**6 F3**
Cross Inn..........3 D4
Cross Inn..........4 F3
Crosshands......2 H3/5 B2
Crosswell......2 H1/3 A6
Crugybar............4 G6
Crundale............2 F3
Crwbin............6 E3
Crymych........2 H1/5 B1
Cwm-Cou............3 C6
Cwm-twrch-isaf......6 H3
Cwmann............4 H6
Cwmbach............5 C2
Cwmbrwy............4 H1
Cwmdu............6 G1
Cwmduad............5 D1
Cwmerfyn............4 H1
Cwmfelin Boeth......2 H3
Cwmfelin Mynach....5 B2
Cwmifor............6 G2
Cwmisfael............6 E3
Cwmllynfell..........6 H3
Cwmorgan............5 C1
Cwmpengraig........3 D6
Cwmsychbant........4 E5
Cwmsymlog..........4 H1
Cwmystwyth..........4 H2
Cwrt-y-cadno........4 H5
Cwrtnewydd........3 E5
Cynheidre..........6 E4
Cynwyl Elfed........5 D1
Dafen............6 F4
Dale............1 D5
Danderwen....2 H2/5 A1
Devil's Bridge........4 H1
Dihewyd............4 E4
Dinas............5 C1
Dinas Cross........2 F1
Drefach............3 D6
Drefach............4 E5
Drefach........**6 F3**
Drefach............6 G3
Drefelin............3 D6
Druidston............2 E4
Dryslwyn............6 F2
Dunvant............6 G5
Dyffryn Ceidrych....6 H2
East Williamston....2 G5
Edwinsford..........6 G1
Efailwen......2 H2/5 A2
Eglwyswen....2 H1/3 A6
Eglwyswrw....2 H1/3 A6
Esgair............5 D1
Felindre............4 F6
Felindre............6 F2
Felindre............6 G4
Felindre Farchog....2 G1
Felinfach............4 F4
Felinfoel............6 F4
Felingwmuchaf......6 E2
Ferryside........**5 D4**
Ferwig............3 B5
Ffair-Rhos..........4 H3
Ffairfach............6 G2
Ffaldybrenin........4 G5
Ffarmers............4 G5
Fforestfach..........6 G5
Ffos-helyg..........4 G2
Ffostrasol..........3 D5
Fishguard........**2 F1**
Five Roads..........6 E4
Foss-y-ffin..........4 E3
Freystrop............2 F4
Garnant........**6 G3**
Gartheli............4 F4
Gelli..........2 G3/5 A2
Gellywen..........5 C2
Glais............6 H5
Glan Denys..........4 F5
Glanbrydan Park....6 G2
Glandwr......2 H2/5 B1
Glandy Cross....2 H2/5 A2
Glanrhyd............3 A6
Glynarthen..........3 C5
Gogian............4 H1
Golden Grove......6 F2
Goodwick........**2 F1**
Gors............4 G1
Gorseinon..........6 F5
Gorsgoch............4 E5
Gorslas........**6 F3**
Gowerton............6 F5
Granston............2 E1

Greynor............6 F4
Grovesend..........6 F5
Gumfreston......2 G5/5 A5
Gumos............6 H4
Gwaun-Cae-Gurwen....6 H3
Gwbert............3 B5
Gwernogle..........6 F1
Gwndwn............4 E6
Gwyddgrug..........4 E6
Halfway............6 G1
Haroldston West....2 E4
Hasguard............2 E4
Haverfordwest....**2 F4**
Hayscastle..........2 E2
Hayscastle Cross....2 E3
Hebron........2 H2/5 B1
Hendy............6 F4
Henllan............3 D6
Henllan Amgoes......2 H3
Henry's Moat........2 G2
Herbrandston........2 E5
Hermon............5 B1
Hermon............5 D1
Hiraeth........2 H3/5 B2
Hodgeston..........2 F6
Hook............2 F4
Horeb............3 D6
Horeb............6 E1
Horton............2 F5
Houghton............2 F5
Hundleston..........2 F6
Ilston............6 F6
Jameson............2 G6
Jeffreyston....2 G5/5 A4
Johnston............2 E4
Jordanston..........2 E2
Keeston............2 E3
Kidwelly............5 D4
Kilgetty....**2 H5/5 A4**
Killay............6 G6
Knelston............6 E6
Lambston............2 E4
Lampeter........**4 F5**
Lampeter Velfry......2 H4
Lamphey............2 F6
Landimore............6 E6
Landore............6 G5
Landshipping........2 F4
Laugharne........**5 C3**
Lawrenny............2 F5
Letterston..........2 F2
Leweston............2 E3
Little Haven........2 E4
Little Newcastle......2 F2
Llan-non............4 F3
Llanafan............4 G2
Llanarth............4 E4
Llanarthney........6 F2
Llanboidy............5 B2
Llanbydder..........4 F5
Llancefn......2 G3/5 A2
Llancrwys............4 G5
Llandawke..........5 C3
Llanddarog............6 E3
Llanddeiniol........4 F2
Llanddeusant........6 H2
Llanddewi............6 E6
Llanddewi Velfry....2 H4
Llanddowror........5 C3
Llandefeilog........5 D2
Llandeilo........**6 G2**
Llandeloy............2 E2
Llandewi Brefi......4 G4
Llandissilio....2 H3/5 A2
Llandovery........**6 H1**
Llandre............4 E6
Llandybie........**6 G3**
Llandyfan............6 G3
Llandyfriog..........3 C6
Llandygwydd........3 B5
Llanegwad..........6 F2
Llanelli............6 E4
Llanfair Clydogau....4 G5
Llanfair-Nant-Gwyn....2 H1
Llanfallteg....2 H3/5 A2
Llanfarian............4 F1
Llanfiangel-ar-arth....4 E6
Llanfihangel-uwch-Gwili....6 E2
Llanfihangel-y-Creuddyn....4 G2
Llanfynydd..........6 F1
Llanfyrnach........5 B1
Llangain............5 D3
Llangathen..........6 F2
Llangeitho..........4 G4
Llangeler............3 D6
Llangendeirne......6 E3
Llangennech........6 F5
Llangennith........5 D6
Llangiwg............6 H4
Llanglydwen....2 H2/5 B2
Llangoedmor........3 B5
Llangolman....2 H2/5 A1
Llangorwen........4 F1
Llangwm............2 F4
Llangwyryfon......4 F2
Llangybi............4 G4
Llangyfelach........6 G5
Llangynin............5 C2
Llanilar............4 G2
Llanllawddog........6 E1
Llanllwch............5 D9

cont.

N

Ynys De

Penclegyr

Porthgain

Abereiddy
Llanrhian
Croes goch

Careg-gwylan fach

Berea

Treglemais

Penllechwen

Carnhedryn

St. David's Head

Treleddyd-fawr

Tretio

B4583

A487

Whitesands Bay

St. David's

Middle Mill

Rhosson

Whitchurch

Solva

A487

msey land

Ramsey Sound

Green Scar

St. Brides Bay

Stacks Rocks

Talben

Tower Point

Skomer Island

Wooltack Point

St. Brides

Marloes

Broad Sound

Gateholm Island

St. Ishmael's

Dale

Dale Point

Skokholm Island

Milfo Have

St. Ann's Head

She Isla

KEY TO MAPS ON PAGES 1-6

Motorway	County boundary
A road	Urban areas
B road	○ ○ Towns/villages
Through road	0 1 2 Miles
Dual carriageway	0 1 2 3 Kilometre

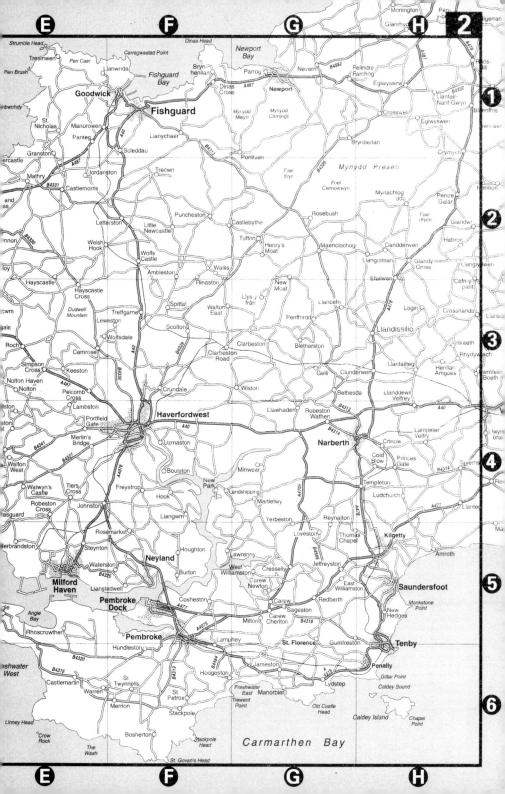

Llanilwni 4 E6
Llanmadoc 6 E6
Llanmiloe 5 C4
Llanmorlais 6 F5
Llannon 5 F4
Llanpumsaint 5 D1
Llanrhian 1 D2
Llanrhidian 6 E6
Llanrhystud 4 F2
Llansadumen 5 C4
Llansamlet 6 H5
Llansantffraed 4 E3
Llansawel 4 G6
Llanstadwell 2 F5
Llanstephan 5 D4
Llanteg 2 H4/5 B4
Llanwenog 4 E5
Llanwinio 5 C2
Llanwnda 2 E1
Llanwnnen 4 F5
Llanwrda 6 H1
Llanybri 5 C3
Llanychaer 2 F1
Llanynog 5 C4
Llawhaden 2 G4
Liechryd 3 B5
Liedrod 4 G2
Lidlad-Nenog 4 F6
Llundain-fach 4 F4
Llwyn-y-brain 5 B3
Llwyn-y-groes 4 F4
Llwyncelyn 4 E4
Llwyndafydd 3 D4
Llys-y-frân 2 G3
Login 2 H3/5 A2
Loughor 6 F5
Loveston 2 G5/5 A4
Luddhurch 2 H4/5 A3
Lydstep 2 G6/5 A5
Maenclochog 2 G2/5 A1
Maescrugiau 4 E6
Maeslyn 3 D5
Maesybont 6 F3
Manorbier 2 G6
Manordeilo 6 G2
Manorowen 2 E1
Margam 6 H6
Marloes 1 D5
Marros 5 B4

Martletwy 2 G4
Mathry 2 E2
Meidrim 5 C2
Merlin's Bridge 2 E4
Merrion 2 F6
Merthyr 5 D2
Middle Mill 1 D2
Milford Haven 2 E5
Milton 2 G5
Minwear 2 G4
Monachty 4 E3
Monington 3 A5
Morfa Bach 5 D3
Morriston 6 G5
Moylgrove 3 A5
Myddfai 6 H1
Mydroilyn 4 E4
Mynachlog-ddu 2 H2/5 A1
Nanternis 3 D4
Nantgaredig 6 E2
Nantycaws 6 E3
Narberth 2 G4/5 A3
Neath 6 H5
Nebo 4 F3
Nevern 2 G1/3 A6
New Hedges 2 H4/5 A4
New Inn 4 E6
New Moat 2 G2
New Park 2 F4
Newcastle Emlyn 3 C6
Newchapel 3 B6
Newchurch 5 D2
Newgale 2 E3
Newport 2 G1
Newton 6 F6
Neyland 2 F5
Nicholaston 6 F6
Nolton 2 E3
Nolton Haven 2 E3
Oakford 4 E4
Oxwich 6 E6
Pant-lasau 6 G5
Panteg 2 E1
Pantglas Hall 6 F2
Pantgwyn 3 B5
Parc-Henri 6 F2
Parcllyn 3 B4
Parkmill 6 F6

Parrog 2 G1
Pelcomb Cross 2 E3
Pembrey 5 D6
Pembroke 2 F5
Pembroke Dock 2 F5
Pen-bont 4 G1
Pen-y-banc 6 G2
Pen-y-bont 5 C2
Pen-y-bont 3 B6
Pen-y-gam 6 E3
Pen-y-groes 6 F3
Penally 2 H5/5 A5
Penant 4 E3
Penbryn 3 C4
Pencader 4 E6
Pencarreg 4 F5
Penclawdd 6 F5
Pendine 5 B4
Penfordd 2 G3
Penharder 3 C6
Penllergaer 6 G5
Penmaen 6 F6
Pennard 6 F6
Penparc 3 B5
Penpurcau 2 F1
Penrhiw-llan 3 D6
Penrhiwpal 3 D5
Penrice 6 F6
Pentre Galar 2 H2/5 B1
Pentre-Gwenlais 6 G3
Pentre-bâch 4 F5
Pentre-cwrt 3 D6
Pentre-llyn 4 G2
Pentrebach 5 D4
Pentrecagal 3 C6
Pentrefelin 6 F6
Pentregat 3 D5
Penuwch 4 F3
Penycwm 2 E3
Plwmp 3 D4
Pont Creuddyn 4 F4
Pont Henry 6 E3
Pont Siân 4 E5
Pont-rhyd-y-groes 4 H2
Pontamman 6 G3
Pontantwn 6 E3
Pontardawe 6 H4
Pontardulais 6 F5
Pontarsais 6 E2

Ponterwyd 4 H1
Pontfaen 2 G1
Pontgarreg 3 D4
Ponthirwaun 3 C5
Pontllw 6 G5
Pontrhydfendigaid 4 H3
Pontrhydyfen 6 H5
Pontyates 6 E4
Pontyberem 6 E3
Port Eynon 6 E6
Port Talbot 6 H6
Portfield Gate 2 E4
Porthgain 1 D2
Porthyrhyd 4 H6
Princes Gate 2 H4/5 A3
Pumpsaint 4 G6
Puncheston 2 F2
Pwll 6 E5
Pwll-trap 5 C3
Red Roses 5 B3
Redberth 2 G5/5 A4
Reynalton 2 G5/5 A4
Reynoldston 6 E6
Rhandirmwyn 4 H5
Rhos 6 H4
Rhos-Hill 3 B6
Rhoscrowther 2 E5
Rhosmaen 6 G2
Rhossili 5 D6
Rhoson 1 C2
Rhyd-Rosser 4 F3
Rhyd-y-fro 6 H4
Rhydargaeau 6 E1
Rhydcymerau 4 F6
Rhydlewis 3 D5
Rhydowen 4 E5
Rhydwrach 2 H3/5 B2
Rinaston 2 F2
Roberton Cross 2 E4
Roberston Wathen 2 G4/5 A3
Roch 2 E3
Rosebush 2 G2/5 A1
Rosemarket 2 G5
Sageston 2 G5
Salem 4 G1
Salem 6 G2
Sandfields 6 H6

Sarnau 5 C2
Saron 6 F3
Saundersfoot 2 H5/5 A4
Scleddau 2 F1
Scolton 2 F3
Scurlage 6 E6
Silian 4 F5
Siloh 4 H6
Simpson Cross 2 E3
Sketty 6 G6
Solva 1 D3
Southgate 6 F6
Spittal 2 F3
Square and Compass 1 D4
St. Brides 1 D4
St. Clears 5 C3
St. David's 1 C2
St. Dogmaels 3 A5
St. Florence 2 G5/5 A5
St. Ishmael 5 D4
St. Ishmael's 1 D5
St. Nicholas 2 E1
St. Petrox 2 F6
St. Twynnells 2 F6
Stackpole 2 F6
Star 5 B1
Steynton 2 E5
Strata Florida 4 H3
Swansea 6 G5
Swyddffynnon 4 G3
Sylen 6 E4
Synod Inn 3 D4
Taibach 6 H6
Tal-sarn 4 F4
Talbenny 1 D4
Talgarreg 3 D5
Talley 6 G1
Talog 5 C2
Tan-y-groes 3 C5
Tavernspite 2 H4/5 B3
Tegryn 5 B1
Temple Bar 4 F4
Templeton 2 H4/5 A3
Tenby 2 H5/5 A5
The Mumbles 6 G6
Thomas Chapel 2 G5/5 A4
Three Crosses 6 F5
Tiers Cross 2 E3
Tonna 6 H5

Trapp 6 G2
Tre-groes 3 D5
Trecwn 2 F2
Trefaen 4 G2
Trefenter 4 G2
Treffgarne 2 F3
Treffynnon 2 E2
Trefin 1 F4
Trefin 1 D2
Tregaron 4 G3
Treglemais 2 E2
Tregoyd 5 C1
Treleddyd-fawr 1 C2
Tremain 3 B5
Tresaith 3 C5
Tresinwen 2 E1
Tretio 1 D2
Trimsaran 5 E4
Troedyraur 3 C5
Tufton 2 G2
Tumble 6 F3
Twynllanan 6 H2
Ty-nant 4 G6
Tycroes 6 G3
Tynygraig 4 H2
Upper Cwm-twrch 6 H3
Upper Killay 6 F6
Uzmaston 2 F4
Wallis 2 F2
Walton East 2 F3
Walton West 1 D4
Walwyn's Castle 2 E4
Warren 2 E6
Waterston 2 F5
Waunarlwydd 6 F5
Welsh Hook 2 E2
West Cross 6 G6
West Williamston 2 G5
Whitchurch 1 D2
Whitland 5 B3
Wiston 2 G3
Wolfs Castle 2 F2
Wolfsdale 2 F3
Yerbeston 2 G5
Ysbyty Cynfyn 4 H1
Ysbyty Ystwyth 4 H2
Ystalyfera 6 H4
Ystrad Aeron 4 F4
Ystradmeurig 4 H3
Ystradowen 6 H3

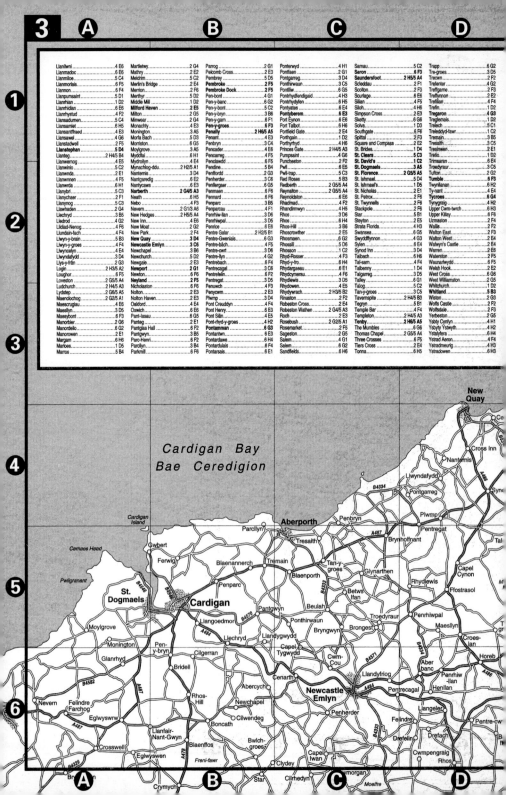

Cardigan Bay
Bae Ceredigion

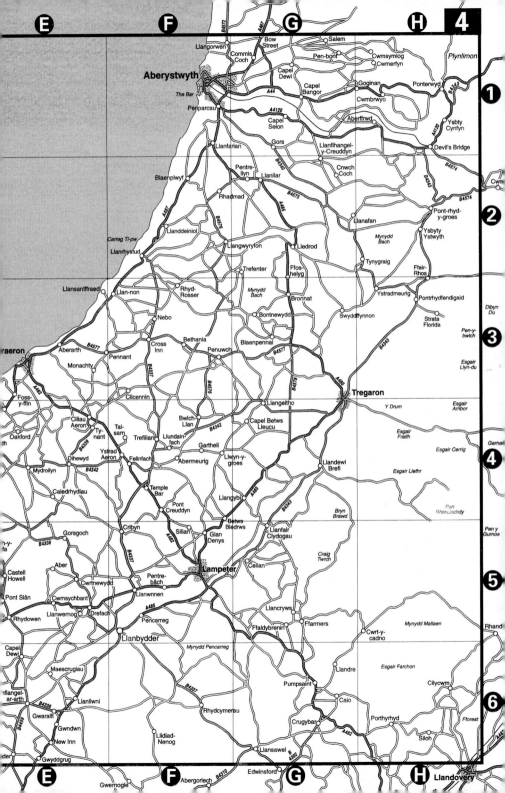

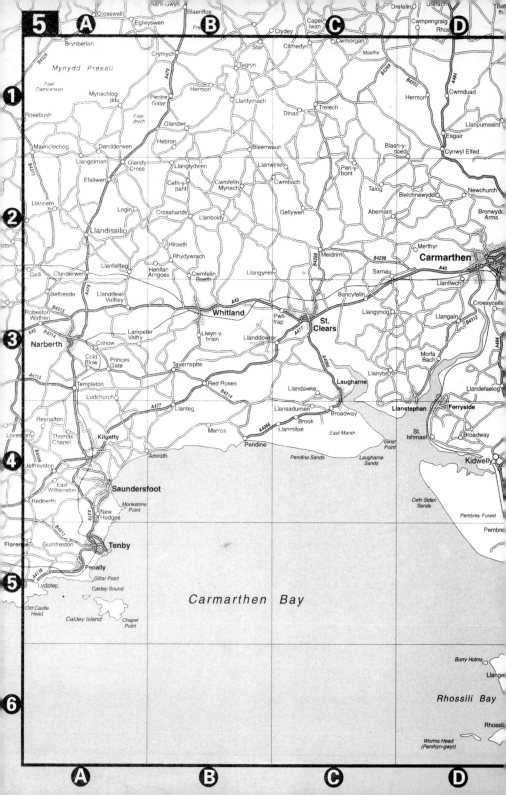

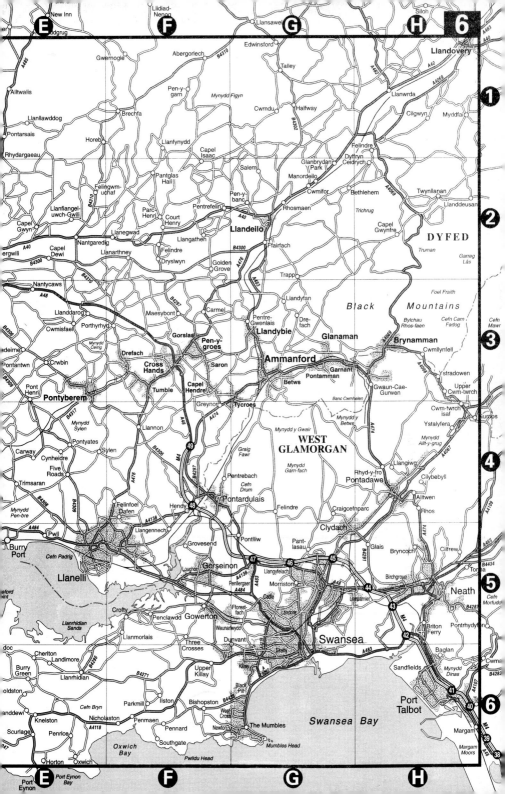

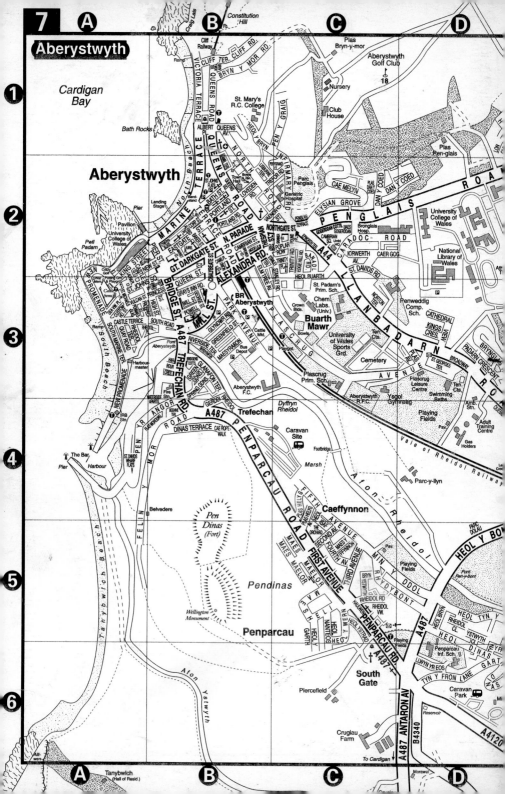

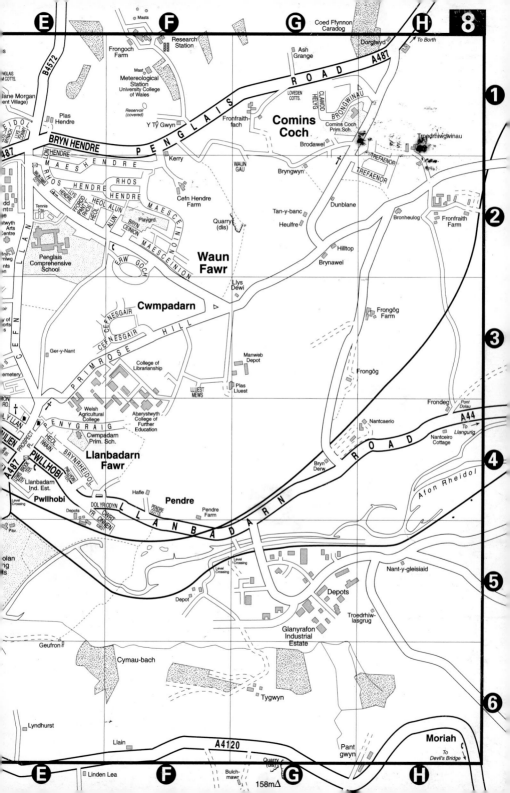

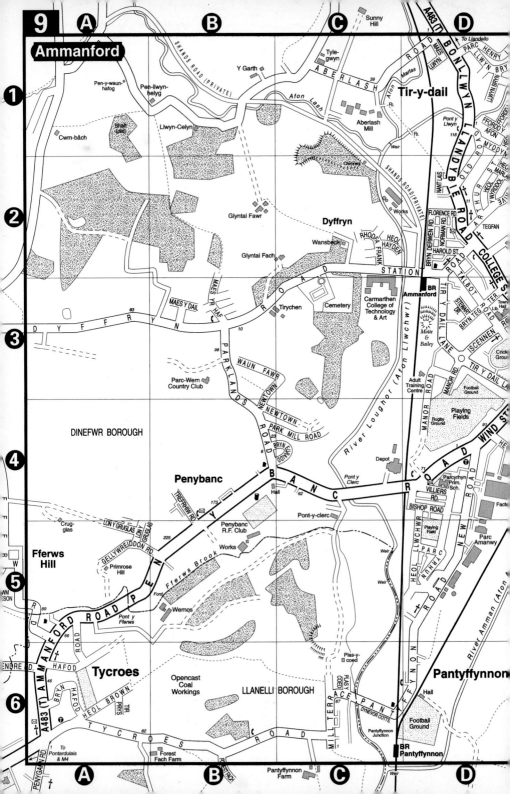

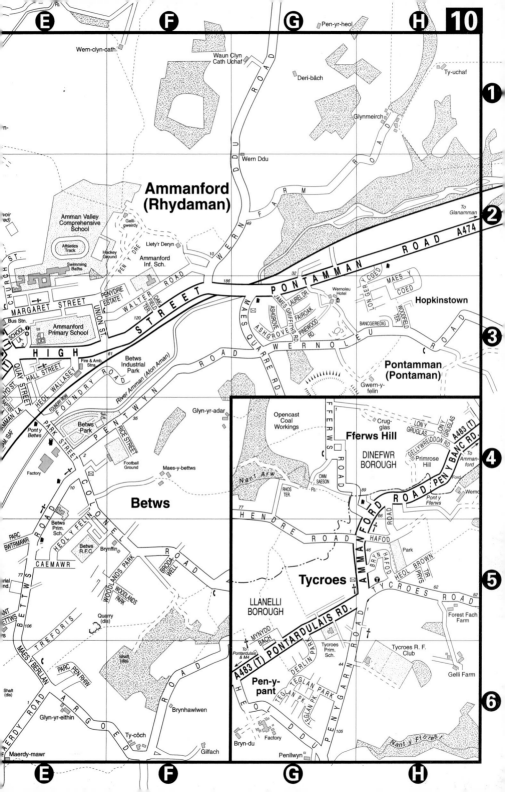

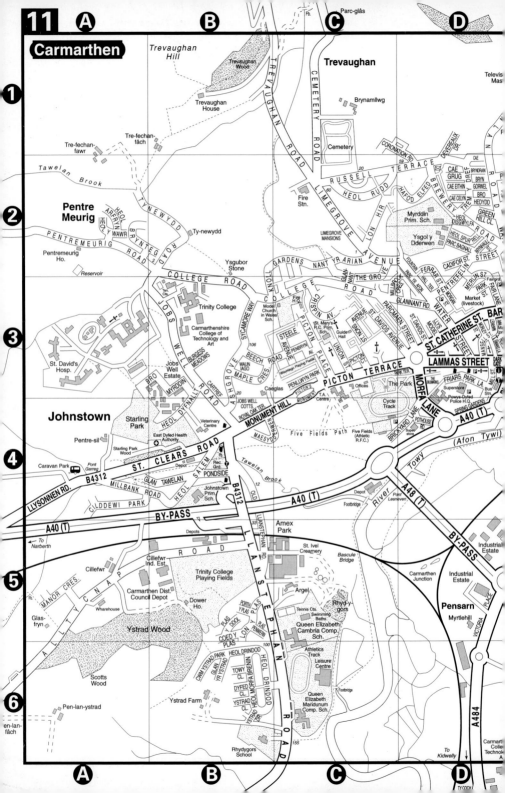

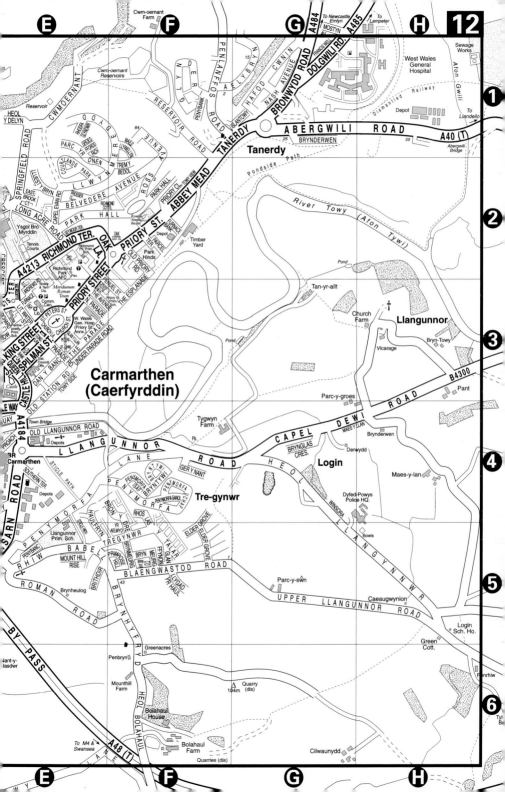

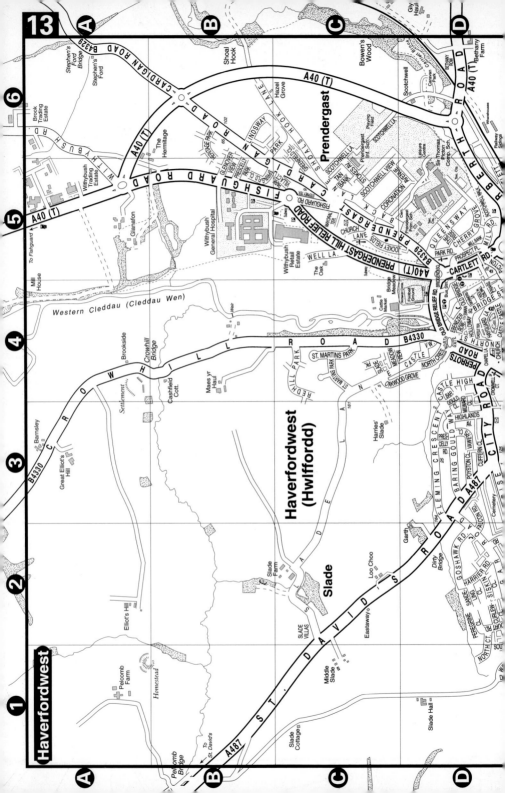

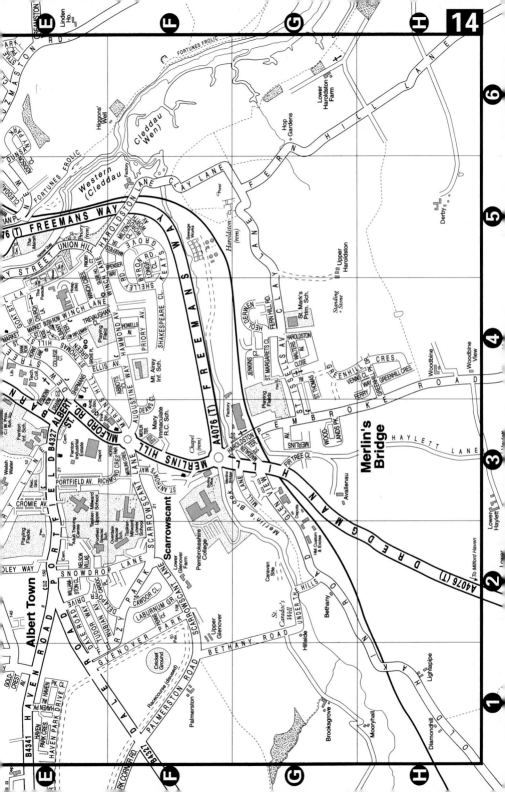

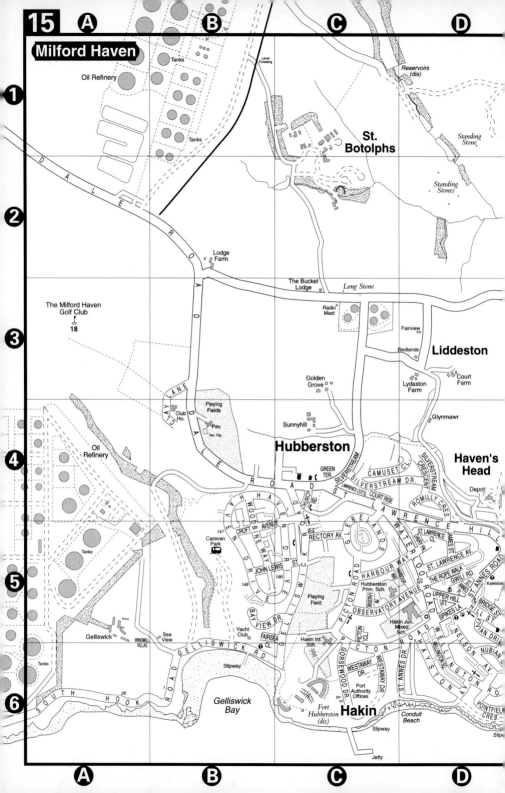

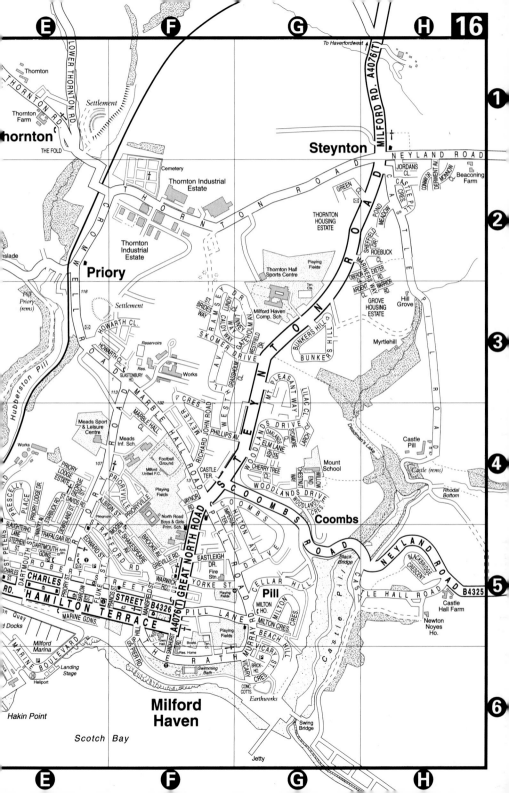

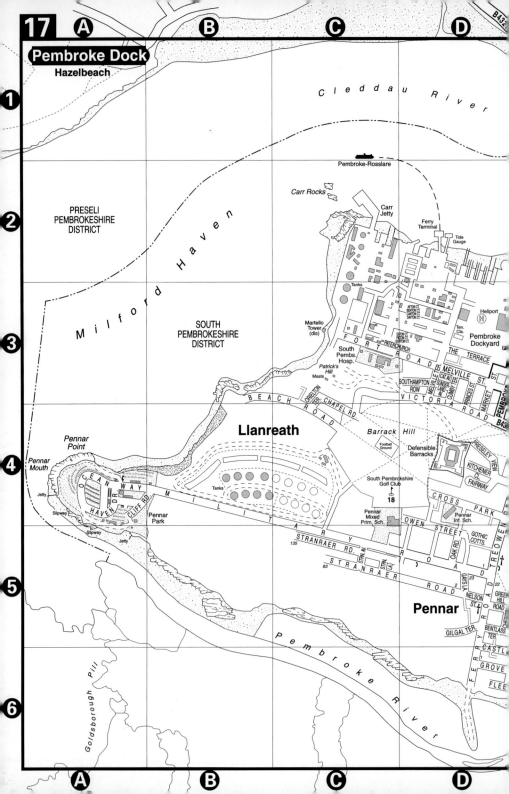

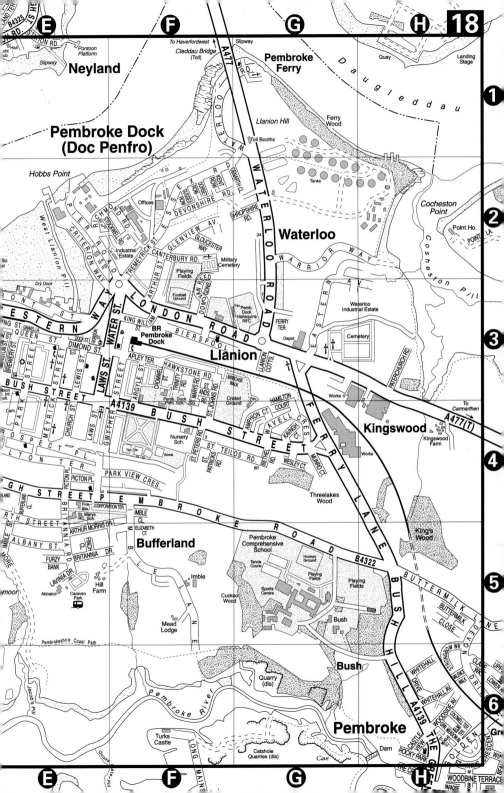

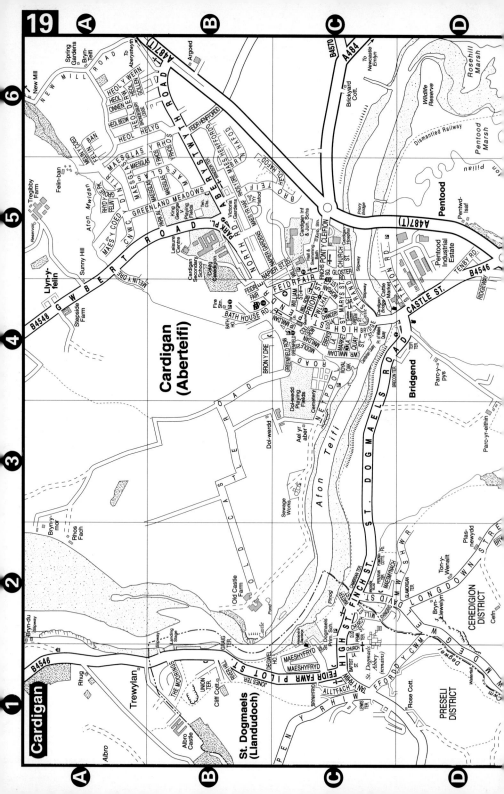

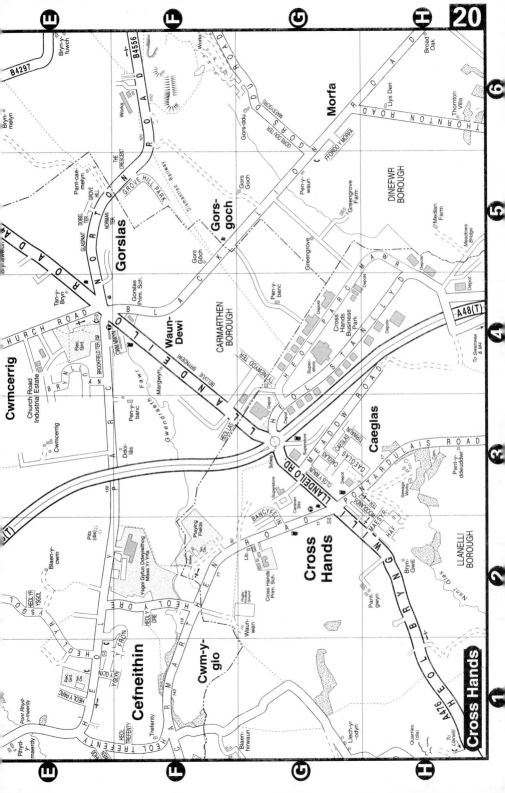

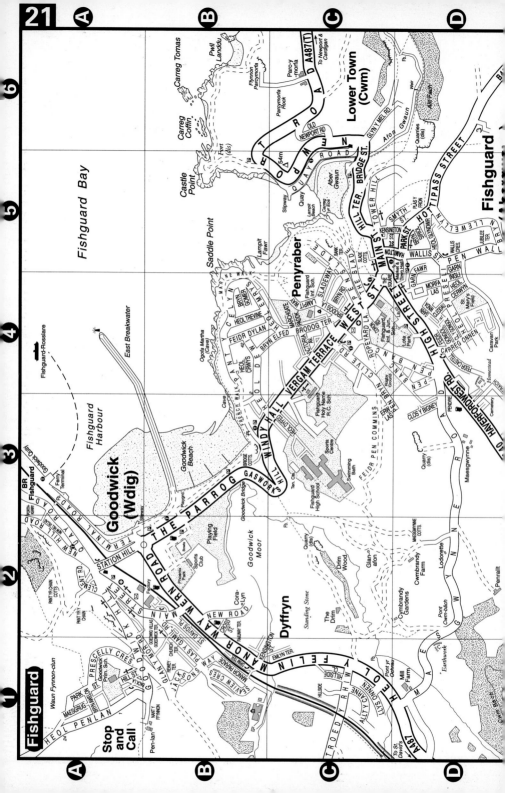

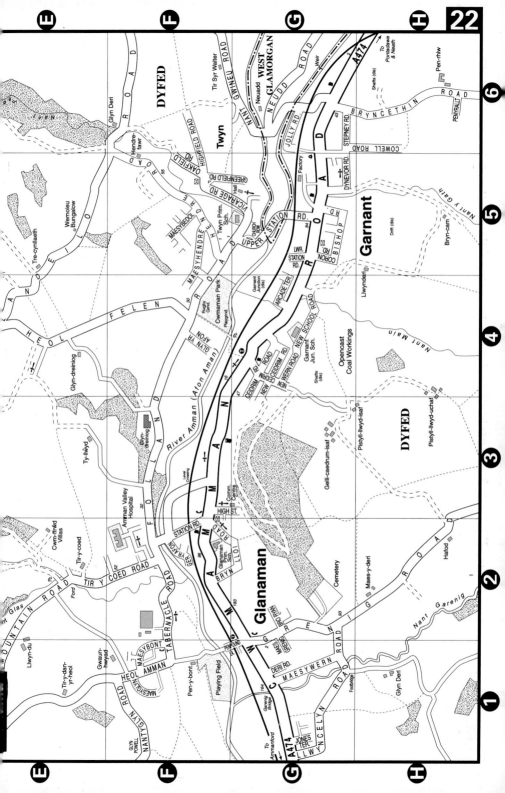

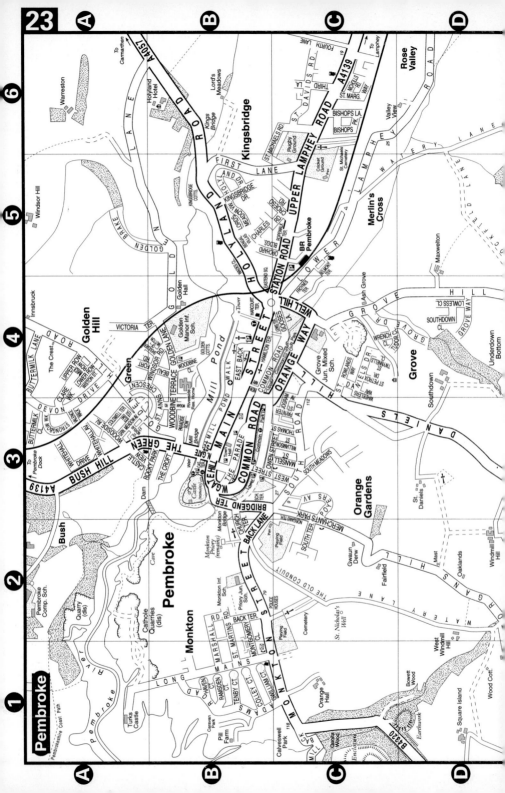

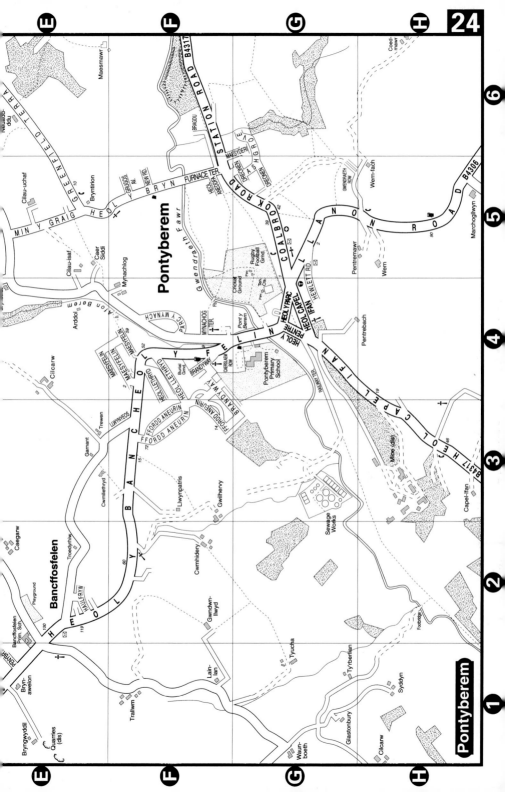

Pontyberem

Bancffosfelen

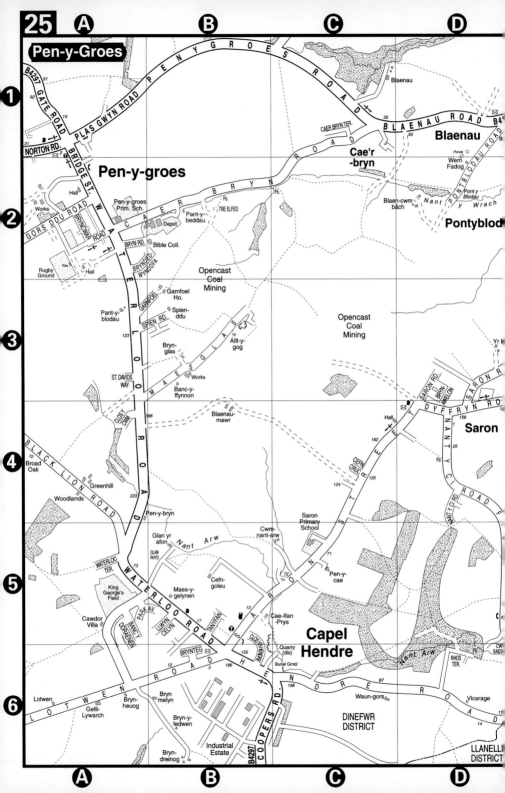

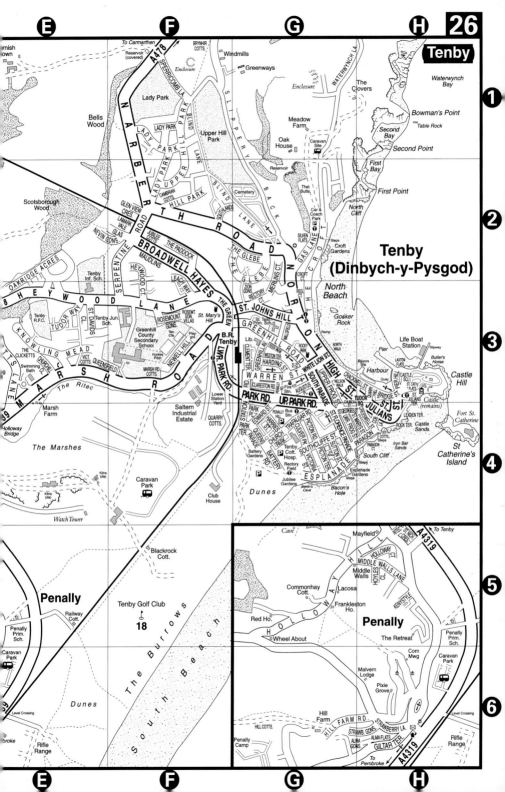

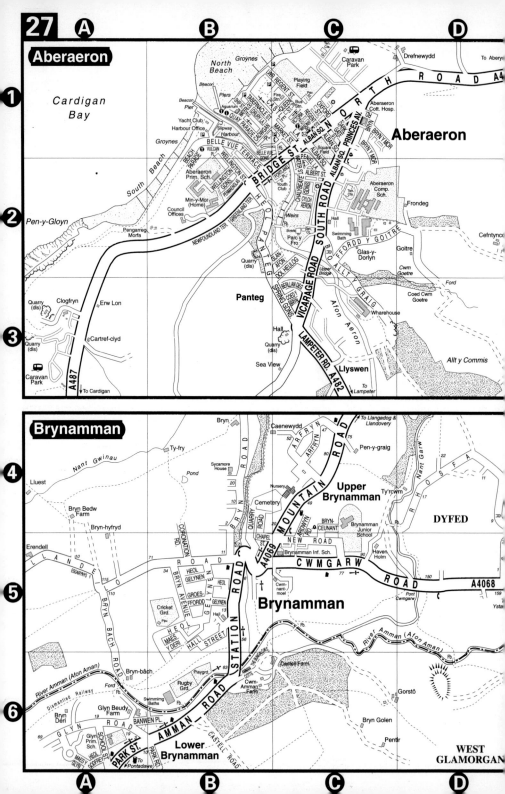

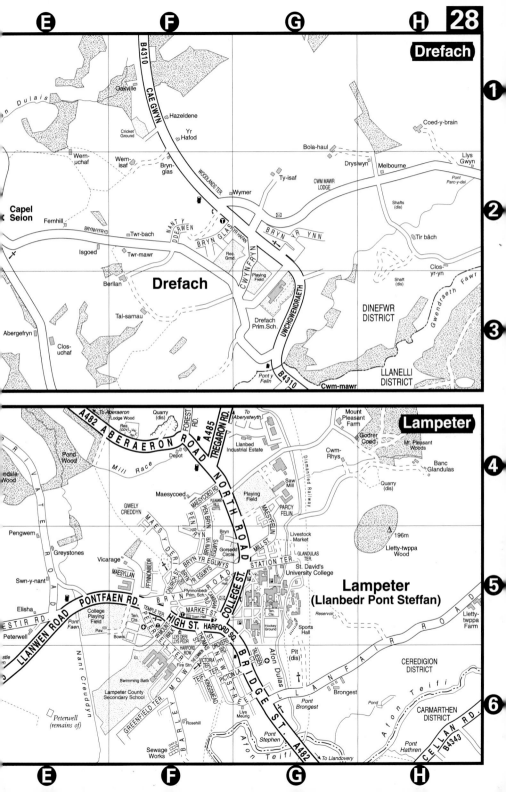

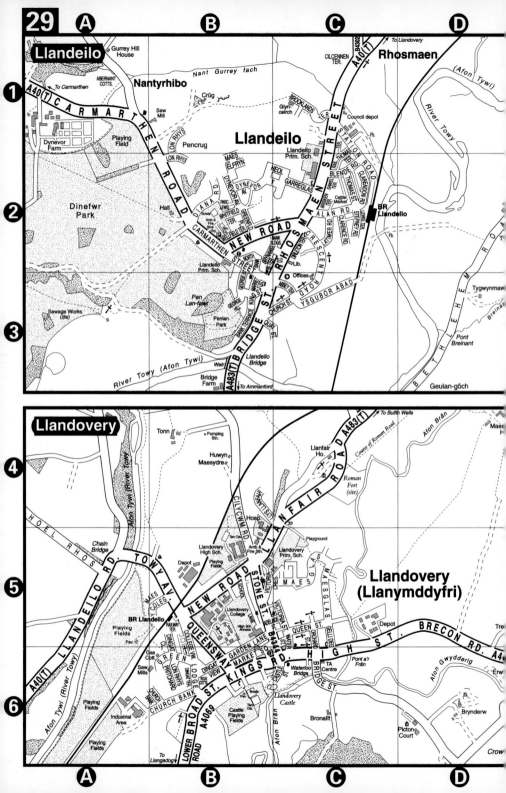

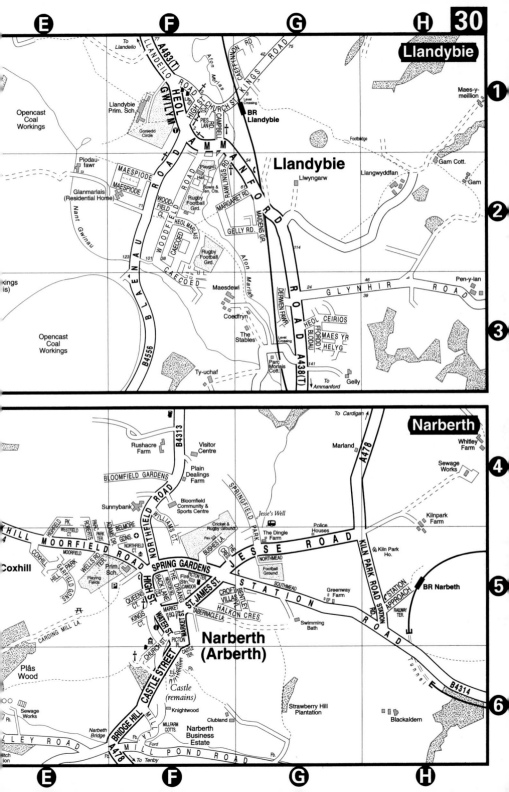

Llandybie

E   F   G   H

1

To Llandeilo

Afon Marlas

KINGS ROAD

CAEFFYNNON RD

77   42   75

A483(T)

Opencast Coal Workings

Llandybie Prim. Sch.

LLANDEILO ROAD

GWLYN HEOL

HIGH ST

CHURCH ST

CAMPBELL

Level Crossing

BR Llandybie

Maes-y-meillion

Gorsedd Circle

PIES LANE RD

Llandybie

2

Piodau-fawr

MAESPIODE

MAESPIODE

Glanmarlais (Residential Home)

Nant Gwinau

WOODFIELD ROAD

WOODFIELD CL.

HEOL MARLAS

Playgrd. Hall

Bowls & Ten. Cts.

Rugby Football Grd.

MARGARET RD

MAIDENS GR.

GELLY RD.

54

61

Llwyngarw

Llangwyddfan

Garn Cott.

Garn

71

MANFORD ROAD

CAECOED

CAECOED

Rugby Football Grd.

114

3

BLAENAU ROAD

CAECOED

123   101   58

Afon Marlas

Maesdewi

Coedfryn

The Stables

Ty-uchaf

DERWEN FAWR

Level Crossing

Parc Morlais Cott.

24

141

GLYNHIR ROAD

46   39

HEOL FFORDD

BLODAU

CEIRIOS

MAES YR HELYG

To Ammanford

Gelly

A438(T)

Pen-y-lan

Opencast Coal Workings

B4556

kings is)

Narberth

E   F   G   H

4

To Cardigan

A478

B4313

Rushacre Farm

Visitor Centre

Plain Dealings Farm

BLOOMFIELD GARDENS

Bloomfield Community & Sports Centre

Sunnybank

NORTHFIELD ROAD

WILLIAMS CT.

SPRINGFIELD PARK

Jesse's Well

Cricket & Rugby Ground

The Dingle Farm

Police Houses

Marland

Whitley Farm

Sewage Works

Kilnpark Farm

5

HILL

MOORFIELD ROAD

HIGHFIELD CT.

WESTFIELD CT.

PK

ROBERTS

BELMORE

ADAMS GDNS.

MOORFIELD

COXHILL

Coxhill

GARFIELD GDNS.

HILL PARK

WELLS RD.

NORTHFIELD CT.

Prim. Sch.

Playing Fields

SPRING GARDENS

THE DRANG

BACK LANE

ST. JAMES ST.

Pew.

BUSHES LA.

NORTHMEAD

Football Ground

JESSE ROAD

SOUTHMEAD

STATION ROAD

Greenway Farm

KILN PARK ROAD

Kiln Park Ho.

STATION APPROACH

BR Narberth

RAILWAY TER.

6

CARDING MILL LA.

Plâs Wood

Sewage Works

HIGH ST.

QUEENS CT.

KINGS CT.

WATER ST.

MARKET ST.

PICTON PL.

CHURCH ST.

Fire Stn.

PICTON TER.

CROFT

VILLAS

BENTLEY

TABERNACLE LA.

HALKON CRES.

CASTLE TER.

Swimming Bath

Narberth (Arberth)

CASTLE STREET

Castle (remains)

Knightwood

MILLFARM COTTS.

Narberth Business Estate

Clubland

Strawberry Hill Plantation

Blackaldern

BRIDGE HILL

A478

MILL POND ROAD

Narberth Bridge

Ford

To Tenby

B4314

LLEY ROAD

itch ion

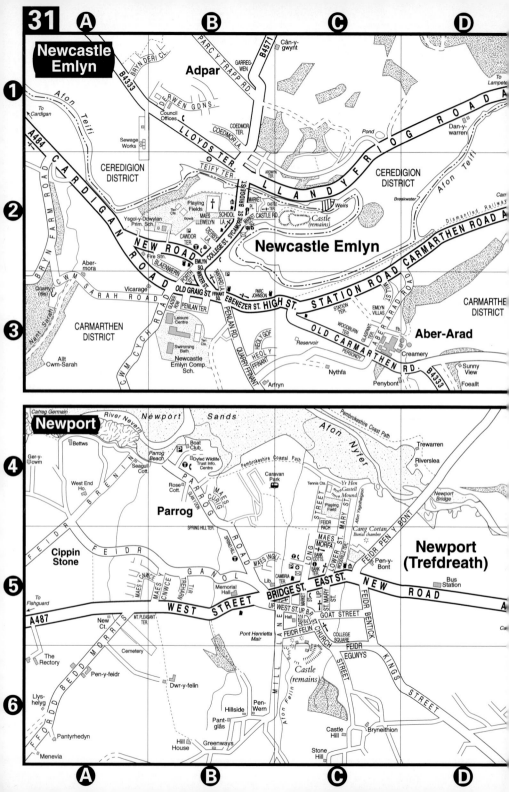

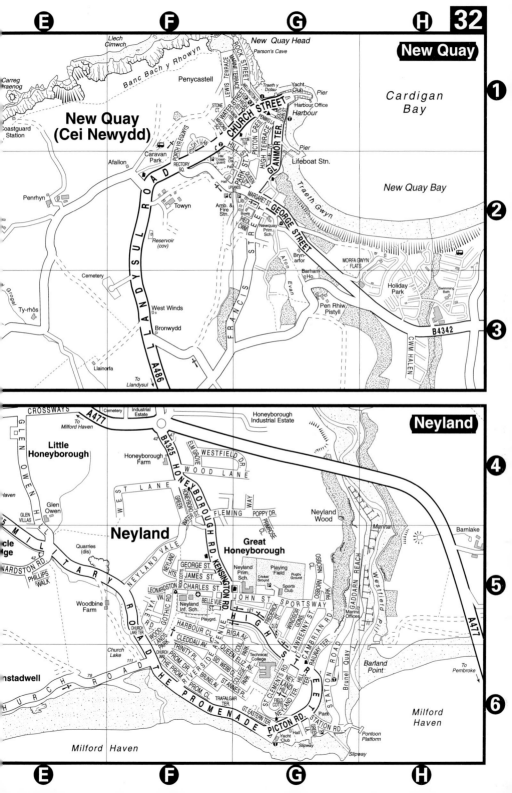

New Quay

E F G H

New Quay (Cei Newydd)

Llech Cimwch
Carreg Graenog
New Quay Head
Parson's Cave
Penycastell
Banc Bach y Rhowyn
Cardigan Bay
1
Coastguard Station
Caravan Park
Afallon
Penrhyn
Towyn
Reservoir (cov)
Cemetery
Ty-rhôs
West Winds
Bronwydd
Llainorfa
To Llandysul
ROCK STREET
LEWIS TERRACE
WATER STREET
STONE CT.
CHURCH STREET
PICTON CRES.
HIGH TERRACE
PENWIG LA.
GLANMOR TER.
RECTORY SQ.
HM Coastguard
UPLANDS
QUAY ST.
PARK ST.
MARGARET ST.
HEOL OWEN
LANDYSUL ROAD
A486
FRANCIS ST.
GEORGE STREET
Lib.
Amb. & Fire Stn.
Newquay Prim. Sch.
Bryn- arfor
Barham Ho.
Afon Evan
Pen Rhiw Pistyll
Traeth y Dolau
Yacht Club
Pier
Harbour Office
Harbour
Pier
Lifeboat Stn.
Traeth Gwyn
MORFA GWYN FLATS
Holiday Park
Swimming Bath
B4342
CWM HALEN
New Quay Bay
Cardigan Bay
2
3

Neyland

E F G H

CROSSWAYS
A477
To Milford Haven
Cemetery
Industrial Estate
Honeyborough Industrial Estate
Little Honeyborough
Honeyborough Farm
B4325
ELM GROVE
WESTFIELD DR.
WOOD LANE
WEST LANE
GREEN
HONEYBOROUGH RD.
WATER ST.
FLEMING
WAY
POPPY DR.
PRIMROSE
Glen Owen
GLEN VILLAS
GLEN OWEN
Haven
MILITARY ROAD
NEYLAND VALE
Quarries (dis)
PHILLIPS WALK
NARDSTON RD.
Woodbine Farm
LEONARDSTON RD.
GOTHIC RD.
NEYLAND HTS.
GEORGE ST.
JAMES ST.
CHARLES ST.
BELLE VUE ST.
Neyland Inf. Sch.
Playgrd.
Church Lake
CHURCH LAKE TER.
HARBOUR CL.
CLEDDAU AV.
GOTHIC LANDS
CHURCH PARK
TRINITY PL.
PROM DR.
AVENUE RD.
KENSINGTON RD.
Great Honeyborough
Neyland Prim. Sch.
Playing Field
Cricket Ground
Sports Club
Rugby Ground
Neyland Wood
Marina
Marine Offices
OSBORN CL.
PARK
GADDARRN REACH
WESTFIELD RD.
Barnlake
JOHN ST.
SPORTSWAY
FREDERICK ST.
WINDSOR GDNS.
CAMBRIAN TER.
RAILWAY TER.
CAMBRIAN RD.
STATION ROAD
Brunel Quay
Marina
Barland Point
To Pembroke
Technical College
RIGA AV.
QUEEN ELIZ.
SID WEBB
ST. CLEMENTS RD.
LAWRENNY
HILL
Park
ncstadwell
CHURCH ROAD
GT EASTERN TER.
THE PROMENADE
TRAFALGAR TER.
PROM CL.
BRUNEL AV.
ST. ANNES PL.
 DUKE ST.
HIGH STREET
PICTON RD.
STATION RD.
FIELD COTTS.
Hall
Yacht Club
Slipway
Pontoon Platform
Slipway
Milford Haven
Milford Haven

4
5
6

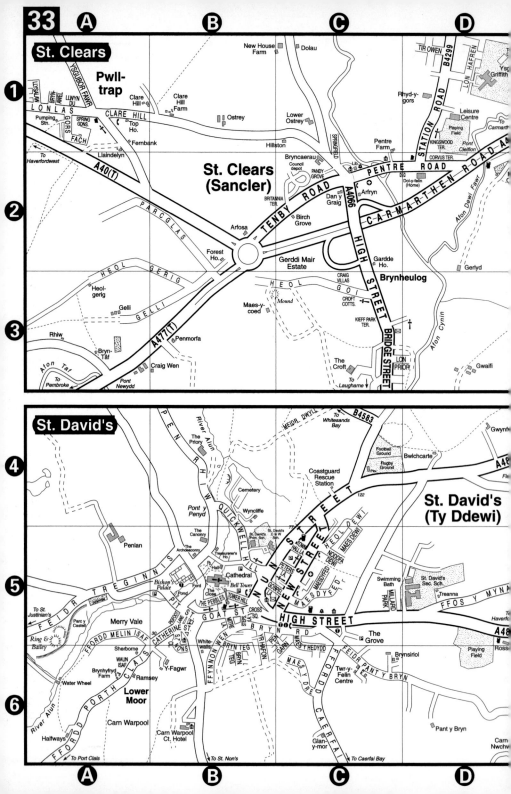

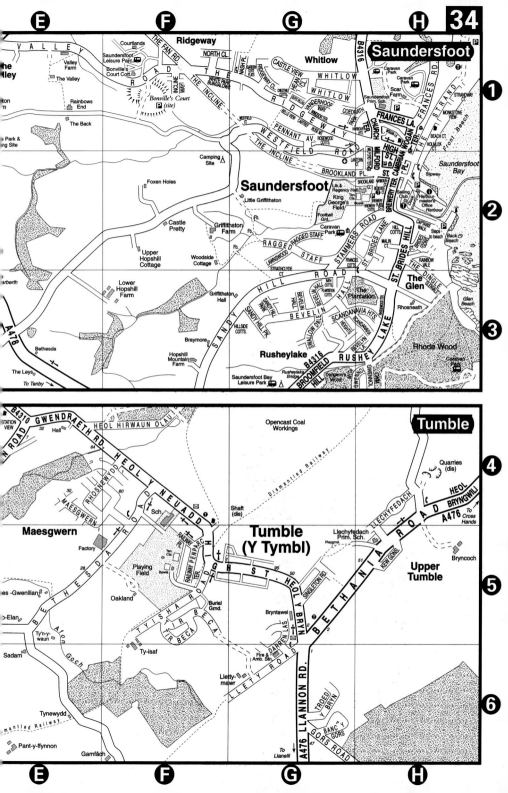

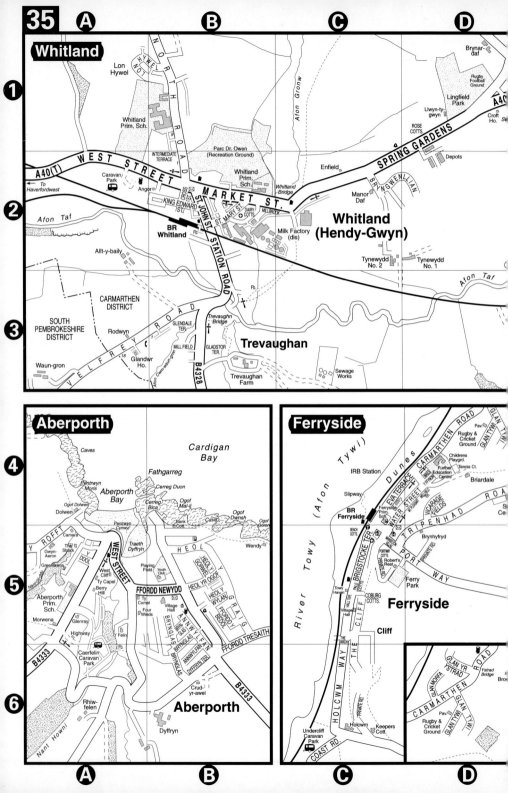

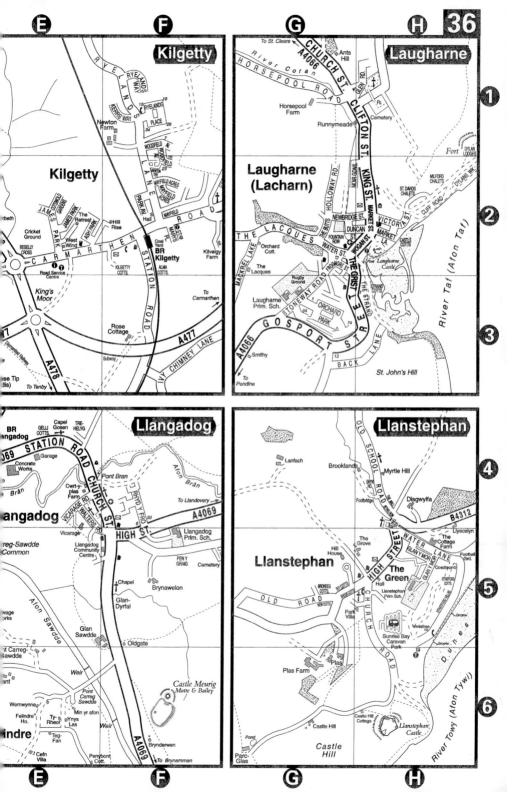

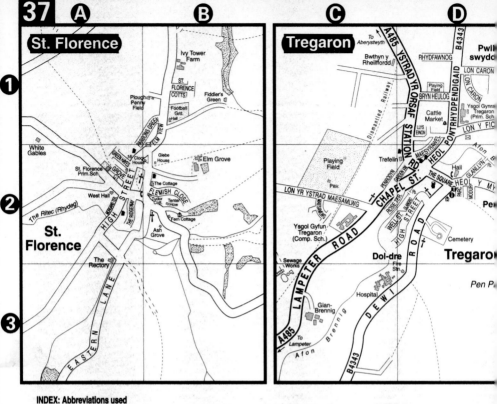

INDEX: Abbreviations used

App.	Approach	Cott(s).	Cottage(s)	Gr.	Grove	Lib.	Library	Rd.	Road
Av.	Avenue	Cres.	Crescent	Grd.	Ground	Lit.	Little	S.	South
Bldgs.	Buildings	Ct.	Court	Grn.	Green	Mark.	Market	Sch.	School
Br.	Bridge	Dis.	Disused	Gt.	Great	Mt.	Mount	Sq.	Square
Bus.	Business	Dr.	Drive	Ho.	House	N.	North	St.	Street
Cara.	Caravan	E.	East	Hosp.	Hospital	Pav.	Pavilion	Stn.	Station
Cem.	Cemetery	Ent.	Enterprise	Ind.	Industrial	Pk.	Park	Ter.	Terrace
Cl.	Close	Est.	Estate	Inf.	Infant	Pl.	Place	Up.	Upper
Comm.	Community	Fb.	Footbridge	Junc.	Junction	Prim.	Primary	W.	West
Comp.	Comprehensive	Gdns.	Gardens	La.	Lane	Rec.	Recreation	Wlk.	Walk

Use of this Index

1. An alphabetical order is followed.
2. Each street name is followed by a map reference giving a page number and coordinates: Albert Street 27 C2.
3. Where a street runs across more than one page the reference number is given: Heol Rheidol 7 D1-8 E1.
4. Where a street name appears more than once the reference is given: Brynglas 35 B5/B6.
5. House numbers along streets are shown: 250.

MYNEGAI: Byrfoddau a ddefnyddir

App.	Dynesiad	Cott(s).	Bwthyn(bythynnod)	Gr.	Llwyn	Lib.	Llyfrgell	Rd.	Heol
Av.	Rhodfa	Cres.	Cilgant	Grd.	Maes	Lit.	Bach	S.	De
Bldgs.	Adeiladau	Ct.	Llys	Grn.	Maes	Mark.	Marchnad	Sch.	Ysgol
Br.	Pont	Dis.	Nis defnyddir	Gt.	Mawr	Mt.	Mynydd	Sq.	Sgwâr
Bus.	Busnes	Dr.	Rhodfa	Ho.	Ty	N.	Gogledd	St.	Stryd
Cara.	Carafán	E.	Dwyrain	Hosp.	Ysbyty	Pav.	Pafiliwn	Stn.	Gorsaf
Cem.	Mynwent	Ent.	Anturiaeth	Ind.	Diwydiannol	Pk.	Parc	Ter.	Teras
Cl.	Clos	Est.	Ystad	Inf.	Babanod	Pl.	Place	Up.	Uchaf
Comm.	Cymuned	Fb.	Pont i gerddwyr	Junc.	Cyffordd	Prim.	Cynradd	W.	Gorllewin
Comp.	Cyfun	Gdns.	Gerddi	La.	Lôn	Rec.	Hamdden	Wlk.	Rhodfa

Sut i ddefnyddio'r

1. Dilynnir trefn yr wyddor.
2. Dilynnir enw pob stryd gan gyfeiriad map yn rhoi rhif tudalen a chyfesurynnau: Albert Street 27 C2.
3. Lle y rhêd stryd dros fwy nag un tudalen rhoddir y cyfeiriad: Heol Rheidol 7 D1-8 E1.
4. Lle ymddengys enw stryd fwy nag unwaith rhoddir y cyfeiriad: Brynglas 35 B5/B6.
5. Dangosir rhifau'r tai ar hyd y strydoedd: 250.

ABERAERON
Population: 1500
Market Day: Wenesday
Alban Square....27 C1/C2
Albert Street....27 C2
Beach Parade....27 B2
Belle Vue Gardens....27 B1
Belle Vue Terrace....27 B1
Berllan Deg....27 C3
Bridge Street....27 B1
Bro Allt y Graig....27 C2
Bryn Road....27 C1
Bryn y Mor....27 C1
Cadwgan Place....27 B1
Castle Lane....27 C1
Chalybeate Gardens....27 C2
Coed y Bryn....27 C3
Dylch Aeron....27 C2
Dark Gate Street....27 C1
Dol Heulog....27 C2
Drury Lane....27 B1
-fordd y Goitre....27 C2
Glanafon....27 B2
Greenland Terrace....27 B2
Heol Panteg....27 C2
Lampeter Road....27 C3
Lower Regent Street....27 C1
Market Street....27 C1
Masons Road....27 C1
Newfoundland Terrace....27 B2
North Road....27 C1
Oxford Street....27 C1
Peniel Lane....27 C1
Penmaenglas....27 B2
Portland Place....27 C2
Princes Avenue....27 C1
Quay Parade....27 B1
Queen Street....27 B1
Regent Street....27 C1
Ship Street....27 B1
South Road....27 C2
Spring Gardens....27 C3
Tabernacle Street....27 B1
Vicarage Road....27 C3
Victoria Street....27 C1
Vulcan Place....27 B1
Water Street....27 C2
Waterloo Street....27 B1
Wellington Street....27 B1

ABERPORTH
Population: 1450
Annwylfan....35 B5/B6
Brynglas....35 B5/B6
Dyffryn Terrace....35 B6
-fordd Newydd....35 B5
-fordd Tresaith....35 B6
-fordd y Bedol....35 B5
Heol y Gorwel....35 B5
Heol y Graig....35 B5
Heol y Wylan....35 B5
Heol yr Ogof....35 B5
Vest Street....35 A5
W Ddol....35 A5
Y Rofft....35 A5

ABERYSTWYTH
Population: 11270
Market Day: Monday
Albert Place....7 B1
Alexandra Road....7 B2
Alfred Place....7 B2
Antaron Avenue....7 D6
Baker Street....7 B2
Banadl Road....7 C2
Beehive Terrace....7 B4
Bilston Terrace....8 E4
Brewer Street....7 B2
Bridge Street....7 B3
Bridgend Cottages....7 B3
Broadway....7 D4
Brongwinau....8 G1
Brook Terrace....8 E4
Bryn Ceinion....8 F2
Bryn Hendre....8 E1
Bryn Rheidol....8 E4
Bryn Ystwyth....7 C5
Bryn y Mor Road....7 B1
Bryn y Mor Terrace....7 B1
Brynglas Road....7 D3
Cae Melyn....7 C2
Cae Rope Walk....7 B4
Caer Gog....7 C2

Cambrian Place....7 B2
Cambrian Square....7 C2
Cambrian Street....7 B2
Cambridge Terrace....7 B2
Caradoc Road....7 C2
Castle Street....7 A2
Castle Terrace....7 A3
Cathedral View....7 D3
Cefn Llan....8 E3
Cefnesgair....8 F3
Chalybeate Street....7 B2
Clawdd Helyg....8 G1
Cliff Road....7 B1
Cliff Terrace....7 B1
Cogerddan Cottages....7 C2
Corporation Street....7 B2
Custom House Street....7 A3
Cwrt yr Onnen....8 E4
Cynffryn Buildings....7 B2
Dan y Coed....7 C2
Dinas Terrace....7 B4
Eastgate Street....7 B2
Edge Hill Road....7 C2
Elm Tree Avenue....7 B2
Elysian Grove....7 C2
Erw Goch....8 F2
Felin y Mor Road....7 A5
Ffordd Pant y Rhos....8 E2
Ffordd Sulien....8 E4
Fifth Avenue....7 C4
First Avenue....7 C5
Fourth Avenue....7 C5
Garth Dinas....7 D6
George Street....7 B3
Gerddi Rheidol....7 A4
Glanrafon Terrace....7 B3
Glanyrafon Industrial Estate....8 G5
Glyndwr Road....7 B3
Grays Inn Road....7 B3
Great Darkgate Street at....7 B2
Green Gardens....7 B3
Greenfield Street....7 B3
Harbour Crescent....7 B3
Haulwen....7 D5
Heol Alun....8 E2
Heol Bryn....7 D5
Heol Dinas....7 D5
Heol Isaf....7 C4
Heol Iwain....8 E4
Heol Nanteos....7 C5
Heol Rheidol....7 D1-8 E1
Heol Tyn y Fron....7 D5
Heol Ystrad....7 C5
Heol y Bont....7 D5
Heol y Bryn....7 B1
Heol y Buarth....7 C2
Heol y Garth....7 C5
Heol y Llan....8 E4
Heol y Wern....7 B3
High Street....7 B3
Infirmary Road....7 C2
Iorwerth Avenue....7 C2
King Street....7 A2
Kings Crescent....7 D3
Laura Place....7 A2
Laurel Place....7 B2
Lewis Terrace....8 E4
Lisburne Terrace....7 B2
Llanbadarn Industrial Estate....8 E4
Llanbadarn Road....7 C3/8 F4
Lluest Mews....8 F3
Llwyn yr Eos....7 D6
Llys Hendre....8 E2
Llys Mynach....8 E1
Lon Cleddau....7 D1
Lon Conwy....8 E1
Lon Dyfi....8 E1
Lon Hendre....8 E1
Lon Teifi....8 E1
Lon Ystwyth....8 E1
Loveden Cottages....8 G1
Loveden Road....7 B2
Maes Ceinion....8 F2
Maes Cogerddan....7 C2
Maes Maelor....7 C5
Maes y Ffynnon....7 C5
Maesheli....7 C5
Maeshendre....8 E2
Maesyrafon....7 B3
Marine Terrace....7 B2
Market Street....7 B2

Mill Street....7 B3
Min y Ddol....7 C5
Moor Lane....7 B2
New Promenade....7 A2/A4
New Street....7 A2
North Parade....7 B2
North Road....7 B1
Northgate Street....7 C2
Norton Terrace....7 C3
Orchard, The....7 C5
Padam Crescent....7 D3
Padam Lane....8 E4
Padam Terrace....8 E4
Parc Dolau....7 C5
Park Avenue....7 B3
Pen y Fron Cottages....8 E3
Pen y Fron Road....8 E4
Pen y Graig....7 C1
Pendre Cottages....8 F4
Penglais Farm Cottages....8 E1
Penglais Road....7 C2/8 F1
Penglais Terrace....7 C2
Penmaes Glas....7 A3
Penparcau Road....7 B4/C5
Pentre Jane Morgan Student Village....8 E1
Penygraig....8 E4
Penygraig Court....7 C2
Pier Street....7 B2
Plas Avenue....7 D3
Plas Dan y Coed....7 C2
Plas Helyg....7 C4
Plas Helyg Avenue....7 C5
Plas Morolwg....7 B4
Plascrug Avenue....7 C3
Poplar Row....7 C2
Portland Road....7 B2
Portland Street....7 B2
Pound Place....7 C2
Powell Street....7 B3
Primrose Hill....8 E3
Princess Street....7 B3
Prospect Place....8 E4
Prospect Street....7 A3
Pwllhobi....8 E4
Pwllhobi Terrace....8 E4
Quay Road....7 A3
Quebec Row....7 D4
Queen Street....7 B3
Queens Avenue....7 B1
Queens Road....7 B1/B2
Rheidol Close....7 D5
Rheidol Place....7 B3
Rheidol Road....7 A3
Rheidol Terrace....7 A3
Rheidol View....7 C5
Rhos Hendre....8 E2
Rhybudd Student Village....8 E2
Rhydybont....7 C5
Rhydyr Afon....7 B3
Riverside Terrace....7 B3
Sea View Place....7 A3
Second Avenue....7 C5
Skinner Street....7 C2
South Marine Terrace....7 A3
South Road....7 B3
Spring Gardens....7 B3
St. Davids Road....7 C2
St. Davids Wharf Flats....7 A4
St. Georges Terrace....7 D4
St. James Square....7 B3
St. Johns Flats....7 B2
St. Johns Square....7 A4
St. Michaels Place....7 A3
Stanley Road....7 C2
Stanley Terrace....7 B2
Swan Square....7 B2
Terrace Road....7 B2
Thespian Street....7 B2
Third Avenue....7 C5
Trefanor....8 F2
Trefechan Road....7 A3
Trefor Road....7 B2
Trinity Place....7 B3
Trinity Road....7 C2
Tyn y Fron Close....7 D6
Tyn y Fron Lane....7 D6
Union Street....7 B2
Vaenor Street....7 B2
Victoria Terrace....7 B1
Vulcan Street....7 A3

Waterside Apartments....7 B3
Waun Fawr Cottages....8 E2
William Street....7 B3
Ystwyth Close....7 D5

AMMANFORD
Population: 10190
Aberlash Road....9 C1
Ammanford Road....9 A6/10 H5
Argoed Road....10 E6
Arthur Street....9 D2
Ashgrove....10 G3
Bancgeredig....10 H3
Baptist Lane....10 E4
Betws Industrial Park....10 F3
Betws Road....10 E5
Bishop Road....9 D4
Bonllwyn....9 D1
Brodawell....10 F5
Bryn Derwen Road....9 D2
Bryn Euraidd....9 C2
Bryn Hafod (Tycroes)....9 A6/10 H5
Bryn Teg Terrace....9 D3
Brynmawr Avenue....9 D2-10 E3
Brynmawr Lane....10 E3
Caemawr....10 E5
Carregamman....9 D4-10 E4
Carregamman Isaf....10 F5
Carregamman Lane....10 E4
Church Street....10 E3
College Street....9 D2
Colonel Road....10 E4
Cwm Saeson (Tycroes)....10 G5
Derlin Park (Tycroes)....10 G6
Dyffryn Road....9 A3-C3
Dynevor Cottages....9 C6
Fairoak....10 G3
Farm Road....10 G2
Fferws Road (Tycroes)....10 G5
Ffordd y Afon....9 D1
Florence Road....9 D2
Forest Fach Estate....9 B6
Foundry Road....10 E4
Foundry Row....10 E4
Gellywreiddon Road (Tycroes)
....9 A5/10 H4
Hafod Road (Tycroes)....9 A6/10 H5
Hall Street....10 E3
Harold Street....9 D2
Heol Brown (Tycroes)....9 A6/10 H5
Heol Ddu (Tycroes)....10 G6
Heol Hayden....9 C2
Heol Las....9 D4
Heol Llwchwr....9 D3
Heol Llwyd....9 D1
Heol Marlais....9 D2
Heol Wallasey....10 E4
Heol y Felin....10 E5
Heol y Wyrddol....9 D2
Iscennen Road....9 D3
James Griffiths Road....10 G3
Laurel Drive....10 G3
Llandybie Road....9 D1
Lloyd Street....10 E3
Llwyn Maes....9 D1
Llwyn y Bryn....9 D3
Lon Ger y Coed....10 H3
Lon y Gruglas (Tycroes)
....9 A5/10 H4
Maerdy Road....10 E6
Maes Quarre Road....10 G3
Maes y Berllan....10 E6
Maes y Coed....10 H3
Maes y Dail....9 B3
Maes yr Haf....9 B3
Manor Road....9 D3
Margaret Street....10 E3
Mill Terrace....9 C6
Myddynfych Drive....9 D1
Mynydd Bach (Tycroes)....10 G5
Nant Lais....9 D2
New Road....9 D5
Newtown....9 B4
Nigh Road....10 D2
Oakfield Terrace....10 F3
Old Road....9 D2
Pant y Bettws....10 E5
Pantyffynnon Road....9 C6
Parc Amanwy....9 D5
Parc Bwtrmawr....10 E5

Parc Henry Lane....9 D1
Parc Pen Rhiw....10 E6
Parcyrhun....9 D5
Park Mill Road....9 B4
Park Street....10 E4
Parklands Road....9 B3
Pen y Banc Road....9 A5-D4/10 H4
Pen y Dre....10 F2
Pentwyn Road....10 E4
Penydre Estate....10 F3
Penygam Road (Tycroes)....10 G6
Pinewood Road....10 G3
Plas y Coed....9 C6
Pont Amman Road....10 G3
Pontardulais Rd. (Tycroes)....10 G6
Quay Street....10 E3
Rhodfa Frank....9 C2
Rhos Terrace (Tycroes)....10 G5
Rice Street....10 F4
School Lane....10 E3
Shands Road....9 B1/C2
Station Road....9 C2
Stewart Drive....9 D3
Talbot Road....9 D3
Tegfan....9 D2
Teglan Park (Tycroes)....10 G6
Tir Prys (Tycroes)....9 A6/10 H5
Tir y Dail Lane....9 D3
Treforis....10 E6
Trefthiw Road....9 B4
Union Street....10 E3
Villiers Road....9 D4
Walter Road....10 F3
Waun Fawr....9 B3
Wern Ddu Road....10 F2
Wernoleu Road....10 G3
Wind Street....9 D4
Woodfield Terrace....10 H3

BRYNAMMAN
Population: 1650
Amman Cottages....27 B6
Amman Road....27 B6
Ardwyn Road....27 C5
Arfryn....27 C4
Banwen Place....27 A6
Bryn Avenue....27 B5
Bryn Bach Road....27 B4
Bryn Road....27 B4
Bryn Seion....27 A6
Brynceunant....27 C4
Bungalows, The....27 B6
Castell Road....27 B6
Chapel Street....27 B5
Coronation Road....27 B6
Cwmgarw Road....27 C5
Esgairynys....27 A5
Glyn Road....27 A6
Groestfordd....27 C3
Hall Street....27 B5
Heol Gelynen....27 B5
Heol Godfrey....27 A6
Llandeilo Road....27 A5-B5
Maes y Deri....27 B5
Maes y Glyn....27 A6
Mountain Road....27 C4
New Road....27 C5
Park Road....27 B6
Park Street....27 A6
Quarry Road....27 B4
Rhosfa Road....27 D4
School Street....27 A6
Station Road....27 B6

CARDIGAN
ABERTEIFI
Population: 3850
Market Day: Saturday
Aberystwyth Road....19 B5
Alltfach....19 C1
Baptist Street....19 C1
Bath House....19 B4
Bath House Road....19 B4
Brecon Terrace....19 C4
Bridge Street....19 C4
Bro Teifi....19 C5
Bron y Dre....19 B4
Brondesbury Lodge....19 A6
Brooklyn Villas....19 B4
Bryn Hafod....19 B5
Bryngwyn....19 D2
Brynhifryd....19 C1
Cambrian Terrace....19 C2
Carriers Lane....19 C4

Castle Street 19 D4
Chancery Lane 19 C4
Church Lane 19 C1
Church Street (Cardigan) 19 C5
Church St. (St. Dogmaels) 19 C2
Cnwc y Dintir 19 A5
College Row 19 C4
Cwmdegwell 19 D1
David Street 19 C2
Degwell House 19 B1
Ebens Lane 19 C4
Feidr Fair 19 B4/C4
Feidr Fawr 19 C1
Feidr Henffordd 19 B6
Felin Ban 19 A5
Ffordd y Cwm 19 C1
Finch Street 19 C2
Finchs Square 19 C5
Glamorgan Terrace 19 D2
Gloster Road 19 C5
Graig Terrace 19 B1
Green Street 19 C4
Greenfield Row 19 C4
Greenfield Square 19 C4
Greenland Meadows 19 A5
Grove Park 19 A5
Gwbert Road 19 A4
Heol Bedw 19 A6
Heol Derw 19 A6
Heol Gollen 19 A6
Heol Hafod 19 A6
Heol Helyg 19 A6
Heol Onnen 19 A6
Heol y Wern 19 A6
High Street (Cardigan) 19 C4
High Street (St. Dogmaels) 19 C1
Jones Terrace 19 B1
Lewis Terrace 19 C1
Longdown Street 19 D2
Lower Mwldan 19 C4
Maes Henffordd 19 B5
Maes y Coed 19 A5
Maes yr Haf 19 B5
Maesglas 19 A5/B5
Maeshyfryd 19 C1
Maesmynach 19 C2
Market Lane 19 C4
Melin y Coed 19 A5
Melin y Dre 19 A4
Middle Mwldan 19 C4
Mill Street 19 C2
Moorings,The 19 B1
Morgan Street 19 C4
Mwtshwr 19 D2
Napier Street 19 B5
Netpool Road 19 C3
New Mill Lane 19 A6
North Road 19 C4
Old Castle Road 19 B2-B4
Park Avenue 19 B5
Park Place 19 B5
Pembroke Terrace 19 C2
Pen y Rhiw 19 C1
Pendre 19 C4
Pentood Industrial Estate 19 C3
Peruvian Terrace 19 C2
Pilot Street 19 C1
Pomona Cottages 19 C2
Pont y Cleifion 19 C5
Priory Street 19 C4
Pwllhai 19 C4
Quay Street 19 C4
Rhos y Dre 19 B5
Rhyd y Felin 19 A5
Ridgeway 19 D4
River Hill 19 B1
Royal Oak 19 C4
Shingrig 19 C2
St. Dogmaels Road 19 C3-D4
St. Mary Street 19 C4
Station Road 19 C4
Strand 19 C4
Tan y Rhiw 19 C1
Teifi Terrace 19 D4
Tenby Road 19 D5
Union Terrace 19 B1
Upper Mwldan 19 C4
Water Street 19 C2
William Row 19 C4
William Street 19 C4
William Terrace 19 C5

Windsor Terrace 19 B5
Y Rhos 19 B6

CARMARTHEN
Population: 14610
Market Days:
Wednesday & Saturday
Abbey Mead 12 F2
Abergwili Road 12 G1
Aelybryn 12 F1
Alltycnap Road 11 A6-12 G1
Amex Park 11 C5
Ash Grove 11 B4
Avenue, The 12 E3
Bank Lane 12 E3
Barn Road 11 D3
Barnsfield Terrace 11 D3
Beech Road 11 B3
Belvedere Avenue 12 E2
Blaengwastod Road 12 F5
Blue Street 11 D3
Brewery Road 11 D2
Brickyard Lane 11 C4
Bridge Street 12 E3
Brithdir 12 E5
Bro Hedydd 11 D2
Bro Myrddin 11 B3
Bron y Dre 12 F4
Bryn Gorwel 11 D2
Bryn Terrace 12 F5
Brynderwen 12 G1
Brynglas Crescent 12 G4
Brynhaul Street 11 D2
Brynhyfryd 12 F5
Brynmeurig 12 F5
Brynteg 11 A2
Bryntywi 12 F4
Bulwarks, The 11 D3
Burgess Meadows 11 B3
Cadifor Steet 11 D2
Cae Bryndrain 11 B4
Cae Celyn 11 D2
Cae Eithin 11 D2
Cae Grug 11 D2
Cambrian Place 11 D3
Capel Dewi Road 12 G4
Capel Evan Road 12 E2
Cartref 11 B3
Castle Hill 12 E3
Cemetery Road 11 C1
Chapel Street 11 D3
Church Lane 12 E3
Church Street 12 E3
Cilddewi Park 11 A4
Coed y Plas 11 B5
College Road 11 B2-C3
Conduit Lane 12 E3
Coracle Way 12 E4
Coronation Road 11 C1
Courtlands Park 12 E2
Cwm Ystrad Park 11 B6
Cwmonenant 12 E1
Dan y Banc 12 E3
Dark Gate 11 D3
Deveraux Drive 11 D1
Dolgwili Road 12 G1
Dyfed Close 11 B6
Eastbrook Court 12 E2
Elder Grove 12 F5
Elliston Terrace 12 E3
Emlyn Terrace 12 E5
Esplanade, The 12 F3
Fair Lane 11 D3
Ferrar Street 11 D2
Five Fields Path 11 D2
Fountain Hall Terrace 11 D2
Francis Terrace 12 E3
Francis Well 12 G1
Friars Park Lane 11 D3
Furnace Bank 12 F2
Furnace Road 12 E3
Ger y Nant 12 F4
Glan Ffynnon 12 F5
Glan Tawelan 11 B4
Glan y Llan 12 E3
Glan yr Ystrad 11 B6
Glannant 11 C3
Glannant Road 11 C3
Glantowy 12 G1
Glynderi 12 F1
Green Hill Close 11 D2
Groesffordd Fach 12 E1

Grove, The 11 C2
Guildhall Square 11 D3
Hafod Cwnin 12 G1
Hafod Elfed 11 D2
Hall Street 12 E3
Haulfryn 12 E4
Heol Arfryn 11 A2
Heol Bolahaul 12 F6
Heol Disgwylfa 11 D2
Heol Drindod 11 B6
Heol Dyfnallt 11 B4
Heol Morfa Brenin 11 B6
Heol Rudd 11 C2
Heol Salem 11 B4
Heol Spurrell 11 D2
Heol y Delyn 12 E1
Heol y Wawr 11 A2
Jacksons Lane 12 E3
Jobs Well Cottages 11 B4
Jobs Well Estate 11 B3
Jobs Well Road 11 B3
John Street 11 D3
King Street 12 E3
Knoll Gardens 11 B3
Lammas Street 11 D3
Limegrove Avenue 11 C2
Limegrove Mansions 11 C2
Little Water Street 12 E3
Llangunnor Road 12 E4
Llanstephan Road 11 B5
Lluest y Bryn 12 E2
Llwynmeredydd 12 E2
Llygad yr Haul 12 F5
Llys Model 11 D3
Llysonnen Road 11 A4
Lon Hir 11 C2
Lon y Plas 11 B5
Long Acre Road 12 E2
Maes Llywellyn 12 F1
Maes y Dderwen 11 B4
Maes y Llan 12 G4
Manor Crescent 11 A5
Mansell Street 11 D3
Maple Crescent 11 B3
Market Way 11 D3
Merlin Lane 11 D3
Merlin Street 11 D3
Mill Street 11 D3
Millbank Road 11 A4
Millbrook Crescent 11 C3
Monument Hill 11 B4
Morfa Lane 11 D3
Morgan Street 11 D3
Morley Street 11 D3
Mostyn Avenue 12 G1
Mount Hill Rise 12 E5
Myrddin Court 12 E3
Myrddin Crescent 12 E2
Nant yr Arian 11 C2
Nash Avenue 12 G1
North Parade 12 E3
Nott Square 11 D3
Oak Cottages 12 F2
Oak Lane 12 E2
Old Llangunnor Road 12 E4
Old Llanstephan Road 11 B4
Old Priory Road 12 F2
Old Station Road 12 E4
Orchard Street 12 E3
Parade Road 12 E3
Parade, The 12 E3
Parc Bagnall 11 D2
Parc Thomas 11 D2
Parc y Delyn 11 D2
Parc yr Afon 11 D3
Parc yr Onnen 12 E1
Parcel Terrace 12 F2
Parcmaen Street 11 C3
Park Hall 12 E2/F2
Park Street 11 D3
Park Terrace 11 D3
Penbryn Avenue 11 C3
Penlan Road 11 D1
Penlanffos Road 12 F1
Penllwyn Park 11 C3
Pensam 12 E5
Pensam Road 12 E5
Pentrefelin Street 11 A2
Pentremeurig Road 11 A2
Penuel Street 12 E3
Penybanc (Pensarn) 12 E5

Penybanc (Tanerdy) 12 E5
Penymorfa 12 F4
Penymorfa Ganol 12 F4
Penymorfa Isaf 12 F4
Penymorfa Uchaf 12 F4
Pibwrlwyd Cottages 12 E6
Pibwrlwyd Lane 11 D6-12 F6
Picton Court 11 C3
Picton Place 11 C3
Pictons Monument 11 C3
Plas Penwern 11 B5
Plas y Ddol 11 B5
Pondside 11 B4
Pondside Path 12 G2
Porth y Plas 11 B5
Pothouse Road 11 D4
Primrose Hill 12 F5
Priory Close 12 F2
Priory Street 12 E3/F2
Prosser Close 12 E2
Quay Street 11 D3
Quay, The 11 D3
Red Street 11 D3
Reservoir Road 12 F1
Rhiw Babell 12 E5
Rhodfa Glyndwr 12 E1
Rhos Las 12 F4
Richmond Cottages 12 E2
Richmond Terrace 12 E2
Roman Road 12 E5
Ross Avenue 12 F1
Royal Oak Terrace 11 B4
Russell Terrace 11 C2
Seymour Terrace 12 E2
Southern Terrace 12 E4
Spilman Street 12 E3
Spring Gardens 11 D4
Springfield Road 12 E2
St. Andrews Road 12 E3
St. Catherine Street 11 D3
St. Clears Road 11 D3
St. Davids Avenue 11 C3
St. Davids Street 11 C3
St. Johns Court 12 E3
St. Mary Street 11 D3
St. Nons Street 11 C3
St. Peters Court 12 E3
St. Peters Street 12 E3
Station Approach 12 E4
Steele Avenue 11 C3
Stephens Way 11 D5-12 E4
Sticle Path 12 E4/E5
Swans Lane 11 D3
Sycamore Way 11 B3
Tabernacle Terrace 11 D2
Tanerdy 12 F1
Towy Close 11 B6
Towy Side 12 F4
Towy View 12 F2
Tregynwr 12 F5
Trem y Dref 12 F2
Trevaughan Road 11 C1
Ty Coch Cottages 11 D6
Tynewydd Road 11 A2
Under Parade Road 12 E4
Upper Llangunnor Road 12 G5
Victoria Place 11 D5
Water Street 11 D3
Waterloo Terrace 11 D2
Waun Iago 11 B3
Wellfield Road 11 D2-12 E2
Winsora 12 G4
Woods Row 12 E3
Y Talar 12 F5
Yr Aelwydd 12 F5
Ystrad Close 11 B6
Ystrad Drive 11 B6

**CROSS HANDS,
CEFNEITHIN &
GORSLAS**
Population: 3080
Bancyfelin 20 G2
Bellvue 20 F4
Black Lion Square 20 F4-H6
Brookfield Terrace 20 E4
Bryndewi 20 F4
Brynlluan 20 E4
Caeglas 20 G3
Carmarthen Road 20 F1-G2
Church Road 20 E4
Clos y Waun 20 G3

Crescent, The 20 F5
Cross Hands Bus. Park 20 G4
Cwm Mwyn 20 F4
Dobel Terrace 20 E5
Ffordd y Morfa 20 G6
Glaspant 20 E5
Gors Ddu Road 20 G6
Gors Ddu Terrace 20 G6
Grove Hill 20 E5
Grove Hill Park 20 F5
Heol Bryngwili 20 G3-H1
Heol Las 20 F3
Heol Parc Mawr 20 G4
Heol Rhos Bowen 20 E1
Heol Stanllyd 20 G3-H4
Heol Trefenty 20 F1
Heol y Dre 20 F2
Heol y Parc 20 E1-E4
Heol yr Ysgol 20 E1/E2
Llandeilo Road 20 E5-G3
Maes yr Haf 20 H2
Maesgors 20 G6
Meadow Road 20 G3
Norman Terrace 20 E8
Norton Road 20 E4-F6
Pontardulais Road 20 G3
Thorton Road 20 H6
Tirwaun 20 G3
Ty Newydd Terrace 20 G4
Woodlands Terrace 20 H3
Y Fron 20 E2
Y Glyn 20 E1

DREFACH
Population: 1000
Bryn Glas 28 F2
Bryn yr Ynn 28 E2
Brynhyfryd 28 E2
Cae Gwyn 28 F1
Cwm Mawr Lodge 28 G2
Cwynfryn 28 G3
Nant y Dderwen 28 F2
Uwchgwendraeth 28 G3
Woodlands Terrace 28 F2
Yr Hafan 28 F2

FERRYSIDE
Population: 1800
Arch, The 35 C5
Beach Cottages 35 C5
Brigstocke Terrace 35 C5
Carmarthen Road 35 D4/D5
Cliff, The 35 C6
Coast Road 35 C6
Coburg Cottages 35 C6
Eva Terrace 35 C6
Glan Tywi 35 D4/D5
Glan yr Ystrad 35 D5
Glanmorfa 35 D6
Hall Terrace 35 C6
Holcwm Way 35 C6
Maes y Ffynon 35 D6
Manselton Villas 35 C6
Mount Pleasant 35 C6
Pale Cottages 35 C6
Port Way 35 D6
Portway Cottages 35 C6
Tripenhead Road 35 C6
Vicarage Fields 35 D6
Water Street 35 C6
Wellfield Terrace 35 C6

**FISHGUARD &
GOODWICK
ABERGWAUN
& WDIG**
Population: 5010
Market Day: Thursday
Allt y Carne ...... 21 C
Back Lane ...... 21 A
Bank Terrace ...... 21 C
Bridge Cottages ...... 21 B
Bridge Street ...... 21 C
Brodog Lane ...... 21 C
Brodog Terrace ...... 21 C
Bryn Awelon ...... 21 A
Bryn Elfed ...... 21 B
Bryn Gomer ...... 21 B
Bryn Llewellyn ...... 21 D
Bryn Road ...... 21 C
Bryn Siriol ...... 21 D
Carreg Onnen ...... 21 D
Church Terrace ...... 21 B
Clement Road ...... 21 A

ive Road....21 C4
los y Bigney....21D3
los y Gongol....21 D4
oronation Road....21 C4
ross Street....21 B2
rim Terrace....21 B1
mlyn Terrace....21 C1
rw Las....21 C3
eidr Castell....21 D4
eidr Dylan....21 B4
eidr Fraich....21 D4
eidr Gongol....21 D4
eidr Pen Commins....21 C3
rench Walk....21 B3
iam Fawr....21 D4
iam Ingll....21 D5
iam Winda....21 D4
iasworks Hill....21 B3
ilan y Mor Road....21 B1
ilyn y Mel Road....21 C6
ioedwick Terrace....21 B2
ioedwig Villas....21 B2
ioodwick Hill....21 B1
iamilton Street....21 D6
iaverfordwest Road....21 D3
ieol Cerwyn....21 D4
ieol Cleddau....21 D4
ieol Cryws....21 B4
ieol Dewi....21 B3
ieol Dyfed....21 C3
ieol Emrys....21 C4
ieol Glyndwr....21 D5
ieol Penlan....21 A1
ieol Preseli....21 C1
ieol Trevine....21 B4
ieol y Felin....21 C1
iligh Street....21 D4
ill Street....21 A1
ill Terrace....21 C5
illside....21 C1
illside Close....21 C1
iottipass Street....21 B1
iacksons Way....21 B1
iubilee Terrace....21 C5
iensington St. (Fishguard)....21 C5
iensington St. (Goodwick)....21 B1
iampit Way....21 C4
iys Onnen....21 C1
iaesgruig....21 A1
iaesgwynne Road....21 D1-D4
iain Street (Fishguard)....21 C5
iain Street (Goodwick)....21 B2
ianor Parade....21 B1
ianor Way....21 B1
iarchgate Paddock....21 C4
iarine Walk....21 D4
iorfa Las....21 D4
ilant y Ffynnon....21 B1
iew Hill Road....21 A2
iew Hill Villas....21 A2
iew Road....21 B2
iewport Road....21 C6
iid Newport Road....21 C6
iant y Celyn....21 B4
iant yr Chain....21 A2
iant yr Chain Cottages....21 A2
iark Sreet (Goodwick)....21 A1
iark Street (Fishguard)....21 D5
iailway Terrace....21 B1
iopeyard Lane....21 C1
iewey Terrace....21 B1
ieaview Crescent....21 B1
iade Cottages....21 C5
iade, The....21 C5
iadeway....21 C4
imyth Street....21 C5
iquare, The....21 C4
it. Davids Place....21 B2
iation Hill....21 A2

Terminal Road....21 A2
Tower Hill....21 C5
Troed y Rhiw....21 C1
Vergam Terrace....21 C4
Victoria Avenue....21C4
Wallis Crescent....21 D5
Wallis Street....21 D5
Wern Road....21 B2
West Street....21 C4
Windy Hall....21 B3

GLANAMAN & GARNANT
Population: 3650
Arcade Terrace....22 G4
Bishop Road....22 G5
Bro Ryan....22 G2
Bryn Lloi Road....22 F2
Bryncethin Road....22 G6
Ceidrim Road....22 G4
Church Row....22 G5
Coronation Road....22 G5
Cowell Road....22 H6
Cwmamman Road....22 G1-G6
Deri Road....22 G1
Dynevor Road....22 G5
Folland Road....22 F2-F5
Ger yr Afon....22 F2
Glyn Powell....22 F1
Glyn yr Afon....22 F4
Greenfield Road....22 G5
Grenig Road....22 G2
Hendre Road....22 F5
Heol Amman....22 F2
Heol Felin....22 E4
High Street....22 F3
Highfield Road....22 F5
Jolly Road....22 G6
Jones Terrace....22 G1
Llandeilo Road....22 E4-F6
Llwyncelyn Road....22 G1
Lower Station Road....22 G5
Maes Grenig....22 G1
Maesybedol....22 F5
Maesybont....22 F1
Maesyglyn....22 F1
Maesyhendre....22 F4
Maesywern Road....22 G1
Mountain Road....22 E1
Nant Gwineu Road....22 G6
Nantyglyn Road....22 G4
Neudd Road....22 G6
New Ceidrim Road....22 G4
New School Road....22 G4
Oakfield Road....22 F5
Penpound Lane....22 F1
Penyrallt....22 H6
Station Road....22 F2
Stepney Road....22 G6
Tabernacle Road....22 F1
Tir y Coed Road....22 E2
Upper Station Road....22 G5
Vicarage Road....22 G5
Wern Road....22 G1

HAVERFORDWEST HWLFFORDD
Population: 13990
Market Day: Saturday
Abbots Close....14 F4
Addison Close....14 E5
Albany Terrace....14 E4
Albert Street....14 E3
Augustine Way....14 F3
Back Lane....13 C5
Bank Row....14 E4
Baring Gould Close....13 D3
Baring Gould Way....13 D3
Barn Street....13 D4-14 E3
Bethany Road....14 F1
Bethany Row....14 E4
Bridge Street....13 D4
Bridgend Square....13 D3
Brook Trading Estate....13 A6
Bush Row....14 F5
Byron Road....14 F5
Cambrian Road....14 E2
Cardigan Road....13 B6-C5
Cardoc Place....14 E2
Cartlett....13 D5
Cartlett Road....13 D5
Castle Back....13 D4
Castle High....13 D4

Castle Square....13 D4
Castle Street....13 D4
Castle Terrace....13 D4
Castle View....13 D4
Cawdor Close....14 F2
Chapel Lane....13 D4
Cherry Grove....13 D5
Church Lane (Centre)....14 E4
Church Lane (Prendergast)....13C5
Church Street....13 D4
City Road....13 D3
Clay Lane....14 F5/G4
Cleddau Avenue....14 E5
Clover Park....14 E6
College Court....14 E4
Coronation Avenue....13 C5
Court Road....13 D2
Creamstone Road....13 D4
Cromie avenue....14 F4
Cromwell Court....13 D4
Crowhill Road....13 A3-C4
Cuffern Close....13 D2
Curlew Close....13 D2
Dale Road....14 E2/F1
Dark Street....13 D4
Deans Close....14 F3
Delapoer Drive....14 F2
Dew Street....14 E4
Douglas James Way....13 D1-14 E1
Drang 14 E3
Dredgman Hill....14 H2
Dunsany Park....14 E6
Ebenezer Row....13 D4
Ellis Avenue....14 E4
Falcon Road....13 D2
Fenton Industrial Estate....14 E3
Fern Hill Lane....14 G5-H6
Fern Hill Road....14 G4
Ferry Way....14 H4
Fir Tree Close....14 H3
Fishguard Road....13 A5-C5
Fleming Crescent....13 D3
Foley Way....14 E2
Fortunes Frolic....14 E6/F6
Fountain Row....14 E2
Freemans Way....14 E5/F4
Friars....14 E1
Furzy Park....14 E1
Gerald Road....13 D2-14 E2
Glebe House....14 E4
Glen View....14 E1
Glenover Park....14 E1
Glenover View....13 B5
Goat Street....14 E1
Goldcrest Avenue....14 E1
Goshawk Road....13 D2
Greenfield Close....13 C5
Greenhill Crescent....14 G4/H4
Greenhill Park Drive....14 H4
Grove Place....14 E4
Hammond Avenue....14 F4
Haroldston Close....13 G4
Haroldston Lane....14 E1
Haroldston Terrace....14 F3
Harrier Road....13 D2
Haven Park Avenue....14 E1
Haven Park Close....14 E1
Haven Park Crescent....14 E1
Haven Park Drive....14 E1
Haven Road....14 E1
Hawthorn Rise....13 D3-14 E2
Hayguard Lane....13 D4
Haylett Lane....14 H3
Heol Derwen....14 G4
Heritage Park....13 B6
High Street....14 E4
Highlands Avenue....14 D3
Hill Lane....14 E4
Hole in the Wall....13 D4
Holloway....13 D4
Homs Lane....14 E4
Horse Fair....14 F3
Howells Avenue....14 E4
Hywel Road....14 G4
Jenkins Close....14 G4
Jockey Fields....13 C5
Jury Lane....13 D4
Keats Grove....14 F5
Kestrel Road....13 D2
Laburnum Grove....14 F2

Lindsway Park....13 B6
Longfellow Close....14 F5
Magdalen Street....14 G3
Mariners Square....13 D4
Market Street....13 E4
Masefield Drive....14 F5
Mayoral Terrace....13 C5
Meadow View....13 C4
Merlin Terrace....14 F3
Merlins Crescent....14 F3
Merlins Hill....14 F3
Milford Road....14 F3
Mill Bank....13 D5
Mill Lane....14 G3
Mill Road....13 D5
Milton Close....14 F5
Milward Close....13 D3
Narberth Road....13 D5
Nelson Villas....14 E4
New Road....14 E5
North Court....13 D1
North Crescent....13 D4
North Gate....13 D4
North Street....13 D4
Nubian Avenue....14 E2
Oakwood Grove....13 C4
Old Bridge....13 D4
Old Bridge Relief Road....13 D4
Old Hakin Road....14 G2-H1
Palmerston Road....14 F1
Park Corner Road....14 F1
Park Road....13 D5
Park Villa Court....13 C5
Pembroke Road....14 G3-H4
Penns Close....14 F2
Peregrine Close....13 D2
Perrot Avenue....13 D4
Perrots Road....13 D4
Picton Place....13 D5
Portfield....14 E2
Portfield Avenue....14 E3
Poyston Close....13 D3
Prendergast....13 D5
Prendergast Hill Relief Rd....13 C5
Prescelly Park....13 B5
Prescelly Road....13 D3
Priory Avenue....14 F4
Prospect Place....13 D5
Quay Street....14 E4
Queen Square....13 D4
Queensway....13 D5
Redhill Park....13 C4
Richmond Crescent....14 E3
Rifleman Lane....14 E4
Rise, The....13 D5
Rosemary Lane....14 E4
Ruther Park....14 E1
Salutation Square....13 D5
Sanderling Close....13 D2
Scarrowscant Lane....14 F2/F3
Scotchwell Lane....13 C5/C6
Scotchwell View....13 C5
Scotchwell Walk....13 D5
Shakespeare Close....14 F4
Shelley Road....14 E4
Shipmans Lane....14 E4
Shoals Hook Lane....13 C6
Siskin Close....13 D2
Skinners Lane....13 D4
Slade Lane....13 C2
Slade Park....13 C2
Slade Villas....13 C2
Snowdrop Lane....14 E2
South Court....13 D1
Spenser Way....14 E4
Spring Gardens....13 D4
Springfield Road....13 B5
St. Anthonys Way....14 F3
St. Davids Road....13 B1-D3
St. Issells Avenue....14 G4
St. Margarets Close....14 G4
St. Martins Court....13 C4
St. Thomas Avenue....14 G4
St. Thomas Green....14 E4
Stepney Terrace....13 C5
Stokes Avenue....13 C5
Style Park....13 E6
Swan Square....13 D4
Tan Bank....13 C5
Tower Hill....14 E4
Trafalgar Close....14 E4

Trafalgar Road....13 D2
Tudor Way....14 E2
Under the Hills....14 G2
Union Hill....14 E5
Upper Market Street....14 E4
Uzmaston Road....14 E6
Vawers Close....13 D3
Venns Close....14 G4
Victoria Road....14 E6
Walters Avenue....14 G4
Well Lane....13 C5
West Court....13 D1
Williamston Close....14 E2
Winch Crescent....14 E4
Winch Lane....14 E4
Windsor Way....14 E5
Withybush Road....13 A5
Withybush Trading Estate....13 A5
Woodlands Park....14 G3
Wordsworth Avenue....14 F5

KILGETTY
Population: 760
Alma Cottages....36 F2
Ash Park....36 E2
Begelly Cross....36 E2
Carmarthen Road....36 E2
Cotswold Gardens....36 F3
Ivy Chimney Lane....36 F3
James Park....36 F1
Kerrs Way....36 F1
Kilgetty Cottages....36 F2
Mayfield....36 F2
Mayfield Acres....36 F2
Newton Terrace....36 F2
Park Avenue....36 E2
Ryelands Lane....36 E1-F2
Ryelands Place....36 F1
Ryelands Way....36 F1
St. Marys Place....36 F2
Station Road....36 F2
Woodfield Avenue....36 F1

LAMPETER LLANBEDRPONT STEFFAN
Population: 1800
Market Day: Tuesday
Aberaeron Road....28 F4
Barley Mow....28 F6
Bridge Street....28 G6
Bryn Road....28 F5
Bryn yr Eglwys....28 F5
Cambrian Road....28 F5
Cellan Road....28 H6
Church Street....28 F5
College Street....28 F5
Common, The....28 F6
Drovers Road....28 F6
Ffynnonbedr....28 F5
Forest Road....28 F4
Glandulais Terrace....28 G5
Greenfield Terrace....28 F4
Gwely Creddyn....28 F4
Harford Row....28 F6
Harford Square....28 F5
High Street....28 F5
Kingsmead....28 F6
Llanbed Industrial Estate....28 G4
Llanfair Road....28 G6
Llanwen Road....28 E6
Llys Deri....28 F5
Llys Pedr....28 F5
Maes y Deri....28 F4
Maestir Road....28 E5
Maesycoed....28 G4
Maesyfelin....28 G4
Maesyllan....28 F5
Market Street....28 F5
Mill Street....28 G5
Mount Walk....28 F6
New Street....28 F6
North Road....28 F4
Parc y Felin....28 G4
Pen Bryn....28 F5
Peterwell Terrace....28 F5
Picton Lane....28 F6
Pleasant Hill Cottages....28 E5
Pontfaen Road....28 F5
St. Thomas Street....28 F5
Station Terrace....28 G5
Taliesen Court....28 G6
Telfi Terrace....28 F6

Temple Terrace ...28 F5
Tregaron Road ...28 F4
Victoria Terrace ...28 F6

LAUGHARNE
LACHARN
Population: 1272

Back Lane ...36 G3
Butts, The ...36 G2
Castle Cottages ...36 H2
Church Street ...36 G1
Cliff Road ...36 H2
Clifton Street ...36 H1
Duncan Street ...36 G2
Dylan Lodges ...36 H1
Dylans Walk ...36 H2
Fountain Row ...36 G2
Frogmore Street ...36 G2
Glen Road ...36 H1
Gosport Street ...36 G3
Grist, The ...36 G2
Holloway Road ...36 G2
Horsepool Road ...36 G1
King Street ...36 H2
Laques, The ...36 G2
Mackrel Lake ...36 G3
Market Lane ...36 H2
Market Street ...36 H2
Milford Chalets ...36 H3
Moir Gardens ...36 G2
Newbridge Street ...36 G2
Orchard Park ...36 G3
St. Davids Chalets ...36 H2
Stoneway Road ...36 G3
Strand Cottages ...36 H3
Strand, The ...36 H3
Victoria Street ...36 G2
Water Street ...36 G2
Wogan Street ...36 H2

LLANDEILO
Population: 2410
Market Day: Saturday

Abbey Terrace ...29 C3
Abernant Cottages ...29 A1
Alan Road ...29 C2
Bank Buildings ...29 C2
Bank Terrace ...29 B3
Bethlehem Road ...29 D3
Blende Road ...29 C2
Bridge Street ...29 B3
Brisken Terrace ...29 C2
Brooklands Terrace ...29 C1
Brynawel Terrace ...29 B2
Carmarthen Road ...29 A1
Carmarthen Street ...29 B2
Church Street ...29 B3
Cilcennen Terrace ...29 C1
Clarence Road ...29 C2
Clarendon Road ...29 C2
Crescent Road ...29 C2
Diana Road ...29 B2
Dirleton Terrace ...29 C2
Dynevor Avenue ...29 B2
George Hill ...29 B3
George Street ...29 B3
Greenfield Place ...29 B2
Heol y Garreglas ...29 C2
King Street ...29 C2
Latimer Road ...29 C2
Lewis Terrace ...29 C2
Lon Rhys ...29 B1/B2
Maes Elfryn ...29 B2
Market Street ...29 B3
New Road ...29 B2
North Bank ...29 B2
Parc Lewis ...29 B2
Quay Street ...29 B3
Railway Terrace ...29 C2
Rhosmaen Street ...29 C2
Sawel Terrace ...29 C2
Station Road ...29 C1
Stepney Road ...29 C2
Thomas Street ...29 B2
Thomas Terrace ...29 B2
Wellfield Terrace ...29 B2
Whitfield Terrace ...29 B2
Ysgubor Abad ...29 C3

LLANDOVERY
LLANYMDDYFRI
Population: 1880
Market Day: Friday

Adelaide Street ...29 C5
Brecon Road ...29 D5
Bridge Street ...29 C6
Broad Street ...29 B6
Castle Street ...29 C6
Church Bank ...29 B6
Cilycwm Road ...29 B4
College View ...29 B5
Dingat Close ...29 B5
Dingat Terrace ...29 B6
Garden Lane ...29 C5
Gelli Deg ...29 C5
Heol Rhos ...29 A4
High Street ...29 C6
Kings Road ...29 B6
Llandeilo Road ...29 A5
Llanfair Road ...29 B4
Llys Llanfair ...29 B4
Lon Rhys Pritchard ...29 B6
Lower Road ...29 B6
Maes y Coleg ...29 B5
Maesglas ...29 C5
Market Square ...29 B5
New Road ...29 B5
Orchard Street ...29 C5
Queen Street ...29 C5
Queensway ...29 B5
Railway Terrace ...29 B5
Rock Cottages ...29 B6
School Lane ...29 B5
Stone Street ...29 B5
Towy Avenue ...29 B5
Victoria Crescent ...29 B5
Victoria Street ...29 B5
Water Street ...29 C5

LLANDYBIE
Population: 2920
Market Day: Tuesday

Ammanford Road ...30 F1-G3
Blaenau Road ...30 F2
Caecoed ...30 F2/F3
Caeffynnon Road ...30 G1
Campbell Road ...30 F1
Church Street ...30 F1
Derwen Fawr ...30 G3
Ffordd y Blodau ...30 G3
Gelly Road ...30 F2
Glynhir Road ...30 G3
Heol Ceirios ...30 G3
Heol Gwilym ...30 F1
Heol Marlais ...30 F1
High Street ...30 F1
Kings Road ...30 G1
Llandeilo Road ...30 F1
Maes yr Helyg ...30 G3
Maespiode ...30 F2
Maidens Green ...30 G2
Margaret Road ...30 F1
Pies Lan ...30 F1
Rawlings Road ...30 F2
Woodfield Close ...30 F2
Woodfield Road ...30 F2

LLANGADOG
Population: 480

Church Street ...36 E4
Gelli Cottages ...36 E4
High Street ...36 F5
Pen y Graig ...36 F5
Rhyd y Fro ...36 E4
Station Road ...36 E4
Trehelyg ...36 E4
Vicarage Road ...36 E4
Walters Road ...36 E4

LLANSTEPHAN
Population: 480

Bethel Row ...36 H4
Bethel Terrace ...36 H4
Brondeg Cottages ...36 G5
Brook Cottages ...36 H4
Bryn House ...36 H4
Church Road ...36 H5
Glan y Mor ...36 H5
High Street ...36 H5
Ivy Cottages ...36 G5
Mill, The ...36 H4
New Cottages ...36 G5
Old Road ...36 G5
Old School Road ...36 H4
Stratford Cottages ...36 H5
Stratford Villas ...36 H5
Water Lane ...36 H5

MILFORD HAVEN
Population: 13470
Market Day: Saturday

Albion Street ...16 E4
Ardent Close ...16 G3
Ash Grove ...16 G4
Barlow Street ...16 E5
Bay View Drive ...15 B5
Beach Hill ...16 G5
Blackbridge Crescent ...16 H5
Brick House ...16 G6
Bridge Street ...15 D5
Brooke Avenue ...16 F5
Bunkers Hill ...16 G3
Caldy Way ...16 F5
Camuset Close ...15 C4
Castle Hall Road ...16 G5
Castle Pill Crescent ...16 H2
Castle Pill Road ...16 H2-H4
Castle Terrace ...16 F4
Cellar Hill ...16 G5
Chapel Street ...16 E5
Charles Street ...16 E5
Cherry Tree Close ...16 G4
Chestnut Way ...16 G4
Church Road ...15 C4
Clay Lane ...15 B4
Concrete Cottages ...16 H2
Conway Drive ...16 H2
Coombs Drive ...16 F4
Coombs Road ...15 C4
Court Rise ...15 C4
Croft Avenue ...16 F5
Cromwell Road ...16 E2-F3
Dairy Park ...15 C4
Dale Road ...15 A2-C4
Dartmouth Gardens ...16 E5
Dartmouth Street ...16 E5
Derwent Avenue ...16 H2
Dewsland Street ...16 E5
Eastleigh Drive ...16 F5
Edward Street ...16 E5
Elm Lane ...16 G4
Exeter Road ...16 F4
Fairsea Close ...15 B5
Fold, The ...16 E1
Francis Street ...16 F5
Fulke Street ...16 E5
Gateholm Avenue ...16 G3
Gelliswick Road ...15 B6/C5
George Street ...16 E4
Glastonbury House ...16 F3
Glebelands ...15 C5
Gorsewood Drive ...15 C6
Grassholm Close ...16 F3
Great North Road ...16 F5
Green Close ...16 G2
Green Terrace ...15 C4
Greville Road ...16 F5
Grove Housing Estate ...16 H3
Gwili Road ...15 D5
Hamilton Terrace ...15 C5
Harbour Way ...15 C5
Haven Drive ...15 B4
Hayston Avenue ...16 G4
Hill Street ...15 D5
Hilton Avenue ...16 G4
Howarth Close ...16 E3
Imogen Place ...16 H5
Imperial Terrace ...16 F4
James Street ...15 D5
John Lewis Street ...15 B5
Jordans Close ...16 H2
Larch Close ...16 G4
Lawrence Cottages ...15 C4
Lilac Close ...16 G3
Linney Way ...16 F3
Lower Thornton Road ...16 E1
Lundy Close ...16 F3
Mable Hall Close ...16 F4
Mable Hall Road ...16 F3
Mansfield Street ...16 F5
Marine Boulevard ...16 E6
Marine Gardens ...16 E5
Mariners Way ...16 H2
Meyler Crescent ...16 F4
Milford Road ...16 H1
Milton Crescent ...16 G5
Milton House ...16 G5
Monnow Close ...16 H2
Mount Pleasant Way ...16 G3
Murray Road ...16 G6
Nelson Avenue ...15 D5
Neyland Road (Coombs) ...16 H5
Neyland Road (Steynton) ...16 H1
Nubian Crescent ...15 D6
Oaklands ...16 G4
Oberon Close ...16 G2
Observatory Avenue ...15 C5
Phillips Avenue ...16 F4
Picton Close ...15 C5
Picton Road ...15 C5/C6
Pier Road ...16 F6
Pill Lane ...16 F5
Pill Road ...16 F4
Point Street ...15 D5/16 E6
Pointfields Crescent ...15 D6
Pond Meadow ...16 H2
Prescelly Place ...16 E4
Priory Lodge Drive ...16 E4
Priory Lodge Estate ...16 E4
Priory Road ...16 E5-F3
Priory Street ...16 E5
Prioryville ...16 F4
Ramsey Drive ...16 F6
Rath, The ...16 F6
Rectory Avenue ...15 C5
Richard John Road ...16 F4
Robert Street ...16 E5
Roebuck Close ...16 H2
Romilly Crescent ...15 D4
Rope Walk, The ...15 D5
Sandhurst Road ...16 F6
Shakespeare Avenue ...16 F5
Sheffield Drive ...16 H2
Silverstream ...15 C4
Silverstream Crescent ...15 D4
Silverstream Drive ...15 C4
Skomer Drive ...16 F3
Slaughterhouse Lane ...16 F5
Slip Hill ...16 F5
South Hook Road ...15 A6
Spikes Lane ...15 D5
St. Annes Drive ...15 D6
St. Annes Place ...15 D5
St. Annes Road ...15 D5
St. Brides Way ...16 F3
St. Davids Road ...16 D4
St. Lawrence Avenue ...15 D5
St. Lawrence Close ...15 D5
St. Lawrence Hill ...15 C4-D5
St. Peters Road ...16 E5
Starbuck Road ...16 E4
Stephen Street ...16 E5
Steynton Road ...16 F4-H2
Stratford Road ...16 E5
Sycamore Close ...16 G4
Thornton Housing Estate ...16 G2
Thornton Industrial Estate ...16 F2
Thornton Road ...16 F2
Trafalgar Road ...16 E5
Upper Hill Street ...15 D5
Upper Thornton Road ...16 E1
Vaynor Road ...16 F4
Vicary Crescent ...16 G6
Vicary Street ...16 G6
Victoria Road ...16 E5
Vivian Drive ...15 D5
Warrior Road ...16 H3
Warwick Road ...16 F5
Waterloo Road ...15 D5
Wellington Gardens ...15 D6
Wellington Road ...15 D5
Wellington Square ...15 D6
Westaway Drive ...15 C6
Westfield Drive ...16 G3
Westhill Avenue ...16 F4
Willow End ...16 G4
Windmill Villas ...15 A5
Woodbine Way ...15 B4
Woodlands Crescent ...16 G4
Woodlands Drive ...16 G4
Yorke Street ...16 F5

NARBERTH
ARBERTH
Population: 1910
Market Day: Thursday

Adams Drive ...30 F5
Back Lane ...30 F5
Belmore Gardens ...30 F5
Bentley Villas ...30 G5
Bloomfield Gardens ...30 F4
Bridge Hill ...30 F6
Bushes Lane ...30 F5
Carding Mill Lane ...30 E5
Castle Street ...30 F6
Castle Terrace ...30 F6
Cawdor Court ...30 F5
Church Street ...30 F6
Coxhill ...30 E5
Crescent, The ...30 E5
Croft Villas ...30 F5
Drang, The ...30 F5
Garfield Gardens ...30 E5
Haikon Crescent ...30 E5
High Street ...30 F6
Highfield Park ...30 E5
Hill Park ...30 E5
Jesse Road ...30 F5
Kiln Park Road ...30 H5
Kings Court ...30 E5
Market Square ...30 E4
Market Street ...30 F5
Mill Lane ...30 F6
Mill Pond Road ...30 F5
Millfarm Cottages ...30 F6
Moorfield ...30 E5
Moorfield Road ...30 E4
Nestor Square ...30 F5
Northfield Court ...30 F5
Northfield Road ...30 F5
Northmead ...30 G5
Parc Roberts ...30 E4
Park Terrace ...30 E5
Picton Place ...30 F5
Picton Terrace ...30 F5
Queens Street ...30 F5
Railway Terrace ...30 H5
Southmead ...30 G5
Spring Gardens ...30 F5
Springfield Park ...30 G4
St. James Street ...30 F5
Station Approach ...30 H5
Station Road ...30 G5/H5
Tabernacle Lane ...30 F5
Valley Road ...30 E6
Water Street ...30 F5
Wells Road Terrace ...30 E5
Westfield Court ...30 E5
Williams Court ...30 F4

NEWCASTLE EMLYN
Population: 1440
Market Day: Friday

Aber Arad Road ...31 C3
Ardwyn Terrace ...31 B2
Blaenwern ...31 B2
Bridge Street ...31 B2
Bryn Deri Close ...31 B1
Bryn Farm Road ...31 A2
Cardigan Road ...31 D2
Carmarthen Road ...31 D2
Castle Road ...31 B2
Castle Terrace ...31 B2
Cawdor Terrace ...31 B2
Coedmor Lane ...31 B1
Coedmor Terrace ...31 B1
College Street ...31 B1
Cwm Cych Road ...31 A3
Cwm Sarah Road ...31 A3
Derby Lane ...31 B2
Derwen Gardens ...31 B1
Ebenezer Street ...31 B3
Emlyn Square ...31 B2
Emlyn Villas ...31 C3
Ffinant Square ...31 B3
Garregwen ...31 B1
Glaspant Terrace ...31 B2
Glazer Row ...31 B1
Heol y Ffinant ...31 B1
Heol y Gof ...31 B2
High Street ...31 B2
Llandyfriog Road ...31 B2-D2
Lloyds Terrace ...31 B1
Maes Llewelyn ...31 B2
Market Place ...31 B2
Market Square ...31 B2
Mill Street ...31 C2
New Road ...31 A2
Old Carmarthen Road ...31 C2
Old Graig Street ...31 B3
Parc Johnson ...31 B3
Parc y Trapp ...31 B2

Penlan Road 31 B3
Penlan Terrace 31 B3
Persondy 31 C3
Porth Street 31 B3
Quarry Ffinant 31 B3
School Lane 31 B2
Station Road 31 C3
Station Terrace 31 C3
Sycamore Street 31 B2
Tanyard Lane 31 B3
Teify Terrace 31 B2
Water Street 31 B3
Woodburn Terrace 31 C3

NEWPORT
Population: 960
Bank Cottages 31 C5
Bank Terrace 31 C5
Bridge Street 31 C5
Cambria Terrace 31 C5
Castle Street 31 C5
Church Street 31 C5
College Square 31 C5
East Street 31 C5
Feidr Bentick 31 C5
Feidr Brenin 31 A5
Feidr Eglwys 31 C4
Feidr Fach 31 C4
Feidr Felin 31 C5
Feidr Ganol 31 A5
Feidr Pen y Bont 31 C5
Ffordd Bedd Morris 31 A6
Glan y Don 31 B4
Goat Street 31 C5
Kings Street 31 C6
Long Street 31 C5
Lower St. Mary Street 31 C5
Maes Curig 31 B4
Maes Ingli 31 B5
Maes Morfa 31 C5
Maes y Cnwce 31 B5
Market Street 31 C5
Mill Lane 31 C6
Mount Pleasant Terrace 31 A5
New Road 31 C5
Parrog Road 31 B4
Spring Hill 31 B5
Spring Hill Terrace 31 B5
Tir Treham 31 B5
Upper Bridge Street 31 C5
Upper St. Mary Street 31 C4
Upper West Street 31 B5
West Street 31 B5
Woodville Terrace 31 C5

NEW QUAY
CEI NEWYDD
Population: 920
Albion Terrace 32 F1
Church Street 32 G1
Cwm Halen 32 H3
Cylch y Llan 32 F1
Francis Street 32 F3
George Street 32 G2
Glanmor Terrace 32 G2
Heol y Cwm 32 G2
High Street 32 G1
High Terrace 32 G2
Hill Street 32 F1
Lewis Terrace 32 F1
Llandysul Road 32 F3
Margaret Street 32 G2
Marine Terrace 32 G1
Masons Square 32 F1
Morfa Gwyn Flats 32 G2
Park Street 32 G2
Penwig Lane 32 G1
Picton Crescent 32 G1
Picton Terrace 32 G1
Porth yr Eglwys 32 F2
Queen Square 32 G2
Rectory Square 32 F2
Rock Street 32 G1
South John Street 32 G1
Stone Court 32 F1
Uplands Square 32 F2
Water Street 32 F1
Wellington Place 32 G1

NEYLAND
Population: 2290
Belle Vue Terrace 32 F5
Brunel Avenue 32 F6
Cambrian Road 32 G6

Charles Street 32 F5
Church Lake Terrace 32 F5
Church Road 32 E6
Church Way 32 F6
Cleddau Avenue 32 F5
College Park 32 G6
Crossways 32E4
Elm Grove 32 F4
Field Cottages 32 G6
Fleming Way 32 F4
Frederick Street 32 G5
Gaddarn Reach 32 G5
George Street 32 F5
Glen Owen Hill 32 E4
Glen Villas 32 E4
Gothic Road 32 F5
Great Eastern Terrace 32 G6
Green Lane 32 G6
Harbour Close 32 F5
High Street 32 G5
Hill Terrace 32 G6
Honeyborough Green 32 F4
Honeyborough Ind. Est 32 F4
Honeyborough Road 32 F4
James Street 32 F5
John Street 32 G5
Kensington Road 32 F5
Lawrenny Street 32 G6
Leonardston Road 32 E5
Leonardston View 32 F5
Military Road 32 E5-F6
Neyland Heights 32 F5
Neyland Hill 32 G6
Neyland Vale 32 F5
Osborn Close 32 G5
Osborn Park 32 G5
Phillips Walk 32 E5
Picton Road 32 G6
Poppy Drive 32 G4
Primrose Close 32 G4
Promenade Close 32 F6
Promenade Drive 32 F6
Promenade, The 32 F6
Queen Elizabeth Avenue 32 F6
Railway Terrace 32 G6
Riga Avenue 32 F5
Riverside Avenue 32 F6
Rock Cottages 32 F5
Sidney Webb Close 32 F5
Sports Way 32 G5
St. Annes Place 32 F6
St. Clements Road 32 G6
Station Road 32 G6
Trafalgar Terrace 32 F6
Trinity Place 32 F6
Vale Road 32 F5
West Lane 32 F4
Westfield Drive 32 F4
Windsor Gardens 32 G5
Wood Lane 32 F4
Woodlands Park 32 F5

PEMBROKE
Population: 7170
Market Day: Friday
Adams Road 23 B1
Back Lane 23 B2
Back Terrace 23 B2
Beaufort Road 23 A4
Belmont Terrace 23 C5
Bengal Villas 23 B5
Bishops Lane 23 C6
Bishops Park 23 C6
Bridgend Terrace 23 B3
Brockfield Lane 23 D5
Bush Hill 23 A3
Buttermilk Close 23 A3
Buttermilk Lane 23 A4
Castle Terrace 23 B3
Castle View 23 A3
Charles Road 23 B5
Church Terrace 23 B2
Clare Walk 23 A4
Coldwell Terrace 23 A3
Colley Court 23 B1
Common Road 23 B3/B4
Croeso Road 23 C5
Croft, The 23 B3
Devon Drive 23 A3
East Back 23 B4
Eastend Square 23 B4
Elm Terrace 23 A3

First Lane 23 B5
Fourth Lane 23 C6
Froynes Terrace 23 C4
Golden Brake 23 B5
Golden Cottages 23 B4
Golden Hill Road 23 A4-B3
Golden Lane 23 A6-B4
Gooses Lane 23 C4
Green Meadow Avenue 23 A3
Green, The 23 B3
Grove Drive 23 D4
Grove Hill 23 C4
Grove Way 23 D4
Gwilliam Court 23 B1
Hamilton Terrace 23 B4
Harcourt Terrace 23 B4
Haven Court 23 B1
Holyland Road 23 B5
Jogram Avenue 23 C3
Kingsbridge Cottages 23 B5
Kingsbridge Drive 23 B5
Lewis Terrace 23 C4
Long Mains 23 B1
Lords Meadow View 23 B5
Lower Lamphey Road 23 C4-D6
Lower Row 23 A4
Lowless Close 23 D4
Main Street 23 B3
Mansell Street 23 C3
Marshall Road 23 B1
Merchants Park 23 C2
Mid Row 23 A4
Mill Brook 23 C1
Mill Pond Walk 23 B3
Monkton Street 23 C1
Montgomery Close 23 B1
New Way 23 B4
Nicholls Road 23 C6
Norgans Hill 23 D2
Norgans Terrace 23 C2
North Gate Street 23 B3
Old Conduit, The 23 C2
Orange Way 23 C4
Orchard Buildings 23 C5
Owen Street 23 B3
Parade, The 23 B3
Paradise Row 23 B3
Paynter Street 23 C3
Police Houses 23 B2
Poyners Avenue 23 C3
Ramsden Court 23 B1
Rocky Park 23 B3
Ropewalk Terrace 23 C5
Rowlands Way 23 C4
School Terrace 23 B3
Shoulder of Lamb 23 B4
South Meadows 23 C3
South Road 23 C3
South Terrace 23 C2
Southdown Court 23 D4
St. Anns Crescent 23 B3
St. Daniels Drive 23 B3
St. Daniels Hill 23 C4-D3
St. Davids Road 23 C6
St. Margarets Way 23 C6
St. Martins Road 23 B1
St. Michaels Road 23 C6
St. Nicholas Close 23 A3
St. Petrox Drive 23 C4
St. Twynnells Close 23 C4
Station Road 23 C4
Strongbow Walk 23 A3
Tenby Court 23 B1
Third Lane 23 C6
Thomas Street 23 C3
Tudor Close 23 C4
Upper Lamphey Road 23 C5
Upper Row 23 A4
Valence Walk 23 A3
Victoria Terrace 23 A4
Wades Close 23 B5
Watery Lane 23 C5/D2
Well Hill 23 C4
West Gate Hill 23 B3
West Street 23 C3
Wheelers Way 23 C4
Whitehall Avenue 23 A3
Whitehall Drive 23 A3
Williamson Street 23 C3
Windsor Road 23 B4
Wiston Street 23 A4

Wogan Road 23 B3
Woodbine Close 23 B4
Woodbine Terrace 23 B3
Woodside Avenue 23 A3
Wrench Close 23 C4

PEMBROKE DOCK
Population: 8650
Afton Court 17 D3
Albany Street 18 E5
Albion Square 18 E3
Amphion Court 18 G4
Apley Terrace 18 F3
Argyle Street 18 F3
Arthur Morris Drive 18 E5
Arthur Street 18 F3
Beach Road 17 B3
Beaufort Road (Pembroke) 18 H6
Belle Vue Terrace 17 D4
Bentlass Terrace 17 D5
Benton Court 17 D3
Bethel Road 18 G4
Bierspool 18 F3
Birdcage Walk 18 F4
Brewery Street 18 E3
Britannia Drive 18 E5
Britannia Road 18 E4
Bufferland Close 18 E4
Bufferland Terrace 18 E4
Bush Hill (Pembroke) 18 H5
Bush Street 18 E3/G4
Buttermilk Cl. (Pembroke) 18 H5
Buttermilk Lane (Pembroke) 18 H5
Canterbury Road 18 F2
Canton Court 17 D3
Carr Terrace 17 D5-18 E6
Castle Street 17 D6-18 E6
Castle View (Pembroke) 18 H6
Catalonia Avenue 17 D3
Cenarth Close 18 G2
Chapel Road 17 C3
Charlton Place 18 E4
Cheriton Road 17 D5
Church Street 18 E4
Clare Walk (Pembroke) 18 H6
Clarence Street 18 E3
Cliff Road 17 A4
Coldwell Ter. (Pembroke) 18 H6
Commercial Row 17 D3
Corporation Terrace 18 E4
Criterion Way 18 E2
Croft Terrace 18 E4
Croft, The (Pembroke) 18 H6
Cromwell Street 18 F3
Cross Park 17 D4
Cumby Terrace 17 D3
Dayton Court 17 D3
Devon Drive (Pembroke) 18 H5
Devonshire Road 18 F2
Dimond Street 18 E3
Dock Street 18 E3
Donovan Reed Gardens 18 F3
Dorset Row 18 F2
Eastern Avenue 18 G3
Eaton Court 17 D3
Elm Terrace (Pembroke) 18 H6
Essex Road 18 F2
Fairway 17 D4
Fenton Court 17 D3
Ferry Lane 18 G4
Ferry Road 17 D6
Ferry Terrace 18 G3
Finch Close 18 E3
Fleet Street 17 D6
Fort Road 17 C3
Front Street 18 E3
Furzy Bank 18 E5
Gays Lane 17 D5
Gilgal Terrace 17 D5
Glenview Avenue 18 F2
Gloucester Way 18 F2
Golden Hill Rd. (Pembroke) 18 H5
Gordon Street 18 E3
Gorton Court 17 D3
Gothic Cottages 17 D5
Gravel Lane 18 E3
Green Meadow Av.(Pemb.) 18 H6
Greenhill Road 17 D5
Grove Street 17 D6-18 E6
Gwyther Street 18 E4
Hamilton Court 18 G4
Haven Drive 17 A4

Hawkstone Road 18 F3
High Street (Neyland) 18 E1
High St. (Pembroke Dock) 18 E4
Hill Street 18 E5
Hill Terrace (Neyland) 18 E1
Imble Close 18 F4
Imble Street 18 E5
Kavanagh Court 18 G4
Kent Row 18 F2
King Street 18 E3
King William Street 18 F3
Kitchener Close 17 D4
Lavinia Drive 18 E5
Laws Street 18 E3/E4
Lewis Street 18 E3
Llanion Cottages 18 G3
London Road 18 F3
Long Mains 18 F6
Lower Row (Pembroke) 18 H6
Market Street 17 D4
Melville Street 17 D3
Melville Terrace 18 E4
Meyrick Street 18 E4
Mid Row (Pembroke) 18 H6
Military Road 17 B4-D4
Milton Terrace 18 E4
Munro Court 18 G4
Nelson Street 17 D5
Neyland Hill (Neyland) 18 H5
Neyland Terrace (Neyland) 18 E1
North Street 18 E4
Oak Road 17 D5
Ocean Way 17 A4
Orielton Terrace 17 C3
Owen Street 17 D4
Paradise Row (Pembroke) 18 H6
Park Street 18 E4
Park View Crescent 18 F4
Paterchurch 17 C3
Paterchurch Road 18 H3
Pembroke Road 18 E4-G5
Pembroke Street 17 D4
Picton Place 18 E4
Picton Road (Neyland) 18 E1
Pier Road 18 E2
Preseley View 17 D4
Princess Street 17 D3
Prospect Place 18 E4
Queen Street 18 E3
Richmond Road 18 E2
Rocky Park (Pembroke) 18 H5
Shropshire Road 18 G2
Southampton Row 17 D3
St. Andrews Road 18 F3
St. Anns Cres. (Pembroke) 18 H6
St. Clements Rd. (Neyland) 18 E1
St. Johns Road 18 F4
St. Marys Road 18 F3
St. Nicholas Cl. (Pembroke) 18 H6
St. Patricks Road 18 F4
St. Peters Road 18 F4
St. Teilos Road 18 F4
Station Road (Neyland) 18 E2
Stockwell Road 18 E2
Stranraer Avenue 17 C5
Stranraer Lane 17 C5
Stranraer Road 17 C5
Strongbow Walk (Pemb.) 18 H6
Sunderland Avenue 17 D3
Sussex Row 18 F2
Sycamore Street 18 E5
Terrace, The 18 F2
Tremeyrick Street 18 F2
Treowen Road 17 D5
Trinity Road 18 F3
Upper Row (Pembroke) 18 H6
Valence Walk (Pembroke) 18 H6
Victoria Road 17 D3
Warrior Way 18 G2
Water Street 18 F3
Waterloo Industrial Estate 18 G4
Waterloo Road 18F1/G2
Wavell Crescent 18 G4
Wellington Street 18 E4
Wesley Court 18 G4
Western Way 18 E3
Whitehall Av. (Pembroke) 18 H6
Whitehall Drive (Pembroke) 18 H6
Windsor Road (Pembroke) 18 H6
Wogan Street (Pembroke) 18 H6
Woodbine Ter. (Pembroke) 18 H6

Woodside Av. (Pembroke).....18 H6

PEN-Y-GROES, CAPEL HENDRE & SARON
Population: 3180

Banc y Ddraenen 25 A5
Black Lion Road 25 A4
Blaenau Road 25 C1
Bridge Street 25 A1
Bryn Road 25 A2
Brynawelon 25 D3
Bryncwar Road 25 A2
Bryndedwynddfa 25 A2
Brynteg 25 B6
Caer Bryn Road 25 A2-C1
Caer Bryn Terrace 25 B1
Cefn Cruc 25 C4
Clos y Cwm 25 A4
Clos yr Hendre 25 B5
Coopers Road 25 B6
Cwm Saeson 25 D6
Dyffryn Road 25 D4
Fferws Road 25 D5
Garnfoel 25 A3
Gate Road 25 A1
Glan Rhyd 25 B5
Gors Ddu Road 25 A2
Hendre Road 25 B6-D6
Llwyn Celyn 25 B5
Lotwen Road 25 A6
Maesglas 25 B3
Nant y Ci Road 25 D4
Norton Road 25 A1
Park Avenue 25 A5
Penygroes Road 25 B1
Plas Gwyn Road 25 A1
Pontblodau Road 25 D2
Rhos Terrace 25 D6
Saron Road 25 D3
Saron Street 25 B5-D4
Spien Road 25 A3
St. Davids Way 25 A3
Tanyfan 25 B5
Tre Elfred 25 B5
Waterloo Road 25 A2-B5
Waterloo Terrace 25 A5

PONTYBEREM
Population: 2620

Ashgrove 24 G5
Bragdu 24 F6
Brandyway 24 F4
Caersalem Row 24 F4
Coalbrook Road 24 G5
Dreonen 24 G5
Ffordd Aneurin 24 F3
Furnace Terrace 24 F5
Greenfield Terrace 24 E5
Grugos Avenue 24 F5
Gwendraeth Row 24 G5
Haulfryn 24 E2
Heol Aneddfa 24 F5
Heol Capel Ifan 24 G4/H3
Heol Llethryd 24 F4
Heol y Banc 24 E2-F3
Heol y Bryn 24 E5
Heol y Felin 24 F3-G4
Heol y Parc 24 G4
Heol y Pentre 24 G4
Howlett Road 24 G4
Llanon Road 24 G5
Llwynyeos 24 F3
Maesyderi 24 F6
Maesyfelin 24 F4
Min y Graig 24 E5
Mynachog Terrace 24 F4
New Road 24 F5
Parc y Mynach 24 F4
Penybryn 24 E1
Railway Terrace 24 G4
Station Road 24 F6

SAUNDERSFOOT
Population: 2680

Bath Cottages 34 G3
Bedoes Court 34 H2
Belle View 34 G1
Bench Court 34 H1
Bevelin Hall 34 G3
Bevelyn Lane 34 H3
Brewery Cottages 34 H2
Brewery Flats 34 H2
Brewery Terrace 34 H2
Brookland Close 34 H2
Brookland Place 34 H2
Broomfield Hill 34 G3
Cambrian Place 34 H2
Captains Walk 34 G1
Cartref 34 G1
Castle View 34 G1
Chestnut Cottages 34 G1
Church Terrace 34 H1
Coedrath Park 34 G1
Cwm Gwennol 34 H3
Dingle, The 34 H3
Fan Road, The 34 F1
Frances Cottages 34 G2
Frances Lane 34 H1
Frances Road 34 H1
Garden Cottage Flats 34 G1
Glenvale 34 H3
Guys Villas 34 G1
Harbour Court 34 H2
Harbour Heights 34 H1
Hean Close 34 G1
High Street 34 H1
Hill Cottages 34 H2
Hillside Cottages 34 G3
Holmlea Court 34 H1
Incline Way 34 F1/G2
Incline, The 34 F1
Lantern Court 34 G1
Lawnswood 34 G2
Malin Court 34 H2
Milford Street 34 H2
Milford Terrace 34 H2
Monkstone View 34 H1
Nash Place 34 G1
North Close 34 F1
Nyth Gwennol 34 G3
Pennant Avenue 34 G1
Plantation Cottages 34 G3
Ragged Staff 34 G2
Rainbow Vale 34 H2
Rhodewood Terrace 34 H3
Ridgeway Close 34 G1
Ridgeway, The 34 F1
Rose Mount 34 G1
Rosewood Cottages 34 G1
Rushey Lane 34 G3
Sandy Hill Park 34 G3
Sandy Hill Road 34 F3
Scandanavia Heights 34 G3
St. Brides Gardens 34 H2
St. Brides Hill 34 H3
St. Brides Lane 34 H2
Stammers Road 34 G2
Stathclyde Court 34 G2
Strand, The 34 H1
Strandway Court 34 H1
Swallow Dale 34 G3
Valley Road 34 E1
Vanderhoof Way 34 G1
Westfield Court 34 G1
Westfield Road 34 G1
White Park Bungalows 34 F1
Whitlow 34 G1
Windsor Terrace 34 G1
Wogan Lane 34 H1
Wogan Terrace 34 H1

ST. CLEARS SANCLER
Population: 1800

Bridge Street 33 C3
Brittannia Terrace 33 B2
Brynawel 33 A1
Carmarthen Road 33 D2
Clare Hill 33 A1
Corvus Terrace 33 D2
Craig Villas 33 C3
Croft Cottages 33 C3
Gelli 33 A3
Gerddi Mair Estate 33 C2
Gors Fach 33 A1
Heol Gerig 33 A3
Heol Goi 33 C3
High Street 33 C2
Kieff Park Terrace 33 C3
Kingswood Terrace 33 D1
Llwyn Du 33 A1
Llysalaw 33 A1
Lon Hafren 33 D1
Lon Prior 33 C1
Lonlas 33 A1
Pandy Grove 33 C2
Parcglas 33 B2
Pentre Road 33 C2
Spring Gardens 33 A1
Springfield 33 C1
Station Road 33 D1
Tenby Road 33 B2
Tir Owen 33 C1
Ysgubor Fawr 33 A1

ST. DAVID'S TY DDEWI
Population: 1460

Bryn Road 33 B5
Bryn Teg 33 B6
Catherine Street 33 B5
Cross Square 33 B5
Feidr Pant y Bryn 33 C6
Feidr Treginnis 33 A5
Ffordd Caerfai 33 C6
Ffordd Melin Isaf 33 A5
Ffordd Porth Clais 33 A6
Ffos y Mynach 33 D5
Ffynnon Wen 33 B6
Goat Street 33 B5
Gospel Lane 33 B5
Heol Dewi 33 C5
High Street 33 C5
Maes Dewi 33 C5
Maes Dyfed 33 C5
Maes y Dre 33 C6
Maes y Hedydd 33 C5
Meidr Dwyll 33 C4
Millard Park 33 C5
Mitre Lane 33 B5
New Street 33 C5
Noddfa Dewi 33 C5
Nun Street 33 B5
Pebbles, The 33 B5
Pen Rhiw 33 B4
Pen y Garn 33 C5
Peters Lane 33 B5
Pigfoot Lane 33 B5
Pit Street 33 B5
Quickwell Hill 33 B4
St. Nons Close 33 B5
Steps Lane 33 B5
Tower Hill 33 B5
Town Hall Lane 33 C5
Waun Isaf 33 A6
Yr Hafon 33 B5

ST. FLORENCE
Population: 470

Eastern Lane 37 A3
Elm View 37 B1
Flemish Close 37 B2
Green Hayes 37 A2
Grove Court 37 A2
High Street 37 A2
Morgans Terrace 37 A2
Parsons Green 37 B1
Ridgeway, The 37 B1
St. Florence Cotts 37 B1

TENBY DINBYCH-Y-PYSGOD
Population: 5630
Market Days: Wednesday & Saturday

Alma Flats (Penally) 26 H6
Alma Gardens (Penally) ...26 G6
Augustus Place 26 G3
Battery Road 26 G2
Blind Lane 26 F1/F2
Bridge Street 26 H3
Broadwell Hayes 26 F2
Brynhir Cottages 26 F1
Cambrian Cottages 26 F2
Castle Square 26 H3
Church Park 26 G4
Church Street 26 G4
Churchill Close 26 E3
Clareston Road 26 G3
Clement Terrace 26 G3
Clicketts Lane 26 E3
Clicketts, The 26 E3
Cob Lane 26 H4
Crackwell Street 26 G3
Cresswell Street 26 H4
Croft Court 26 G2
Croft, The 26 G3
Culver Park 26 G4
Deer Park 26 G3
Edward Street 26 G4
Esplanade 26 G4
Giltar Terrace (Penally) .26 H6
Gas Lane 26 G2
Glas Nevin Gardens 26 F2
Glebe, The 26 G2
Glen View Crescent 26 F2
Green, The 26 F3
Greenhill Avenue 26 G3
Greenhill Road 26 G3
Harding Street 26 G3
Harries Street 26 G4
Heywood Court 26 F2
High Street 26 G3
Hill Cottages (Penally) ..26 G6
Hill Farm Road (Penally) .26 G3
Hill Park 26 G4
Holloway Court (Penally) .26 H5
Holloway Hill (Penally) ..26 G5
Hoyles Close (Penally) ...26 H5
Ivy Cottages 26 H4
Jubilee Cottages 26 F2
Kenystyle (Penally) 26 H5
Knowling Mead 26 E3
Lady Park 26 F1/F2
Lamark Vale 26 F2
Laxton Flats 26 H3
Leach Way 26 F2
Lexden Terrace 26 H4
Lower Frog Street 26 G4
Lower Park Road 26 F3
Marsh Road 26 E3
Marsh Road Cottages 26 F3
Maudlins 26 F2
Merlins Court 26 G3
Middle Walls Lane (Penally) ..26 H5
Narberth Road 26 F1-G2
Nelson Walk 26 F3
Newell Hill 26 F3
Newood Lane 26 E3
North Walk 26 G3
Norton 26 G2
Oakridge Acres 26 E3
Paddock, The 26 F2
Paragon 26 H4
Paragon Court 26 H4
Park Place 26 G4
Park Road 26 G4
Park Terrace 26 G4
Penally Hill 26 G4
Penally Road 26 G3
Picton Road 26 G4
Picton Terrace 26 G4
Pier Hill 26 H3
Quarry Cottages 26 G4
Quay Hill 26 H3
Queens Parade 26 G4
Queensfield 26 E3
Rectory Court 26 G4
Regency Court 26 G3
Ritec Row (Penally) 26 H5
Rock Terrace 26 H4
Rocky Park 26 G3
Rosemount Garden Villas ..26 F3
Rosemount Gardens 26 F3
Saltern Industrial Estate .26 F4
Serpentine Road 26 F3
Silven Flats 26 G2
Slippery Back 26 F3
South Parade 26 G3
Southcliffe Street 26 G4
Southlands 26 F2
Spericomb Lane 26 F1
St. Catherines Flats 26 H3
St. Davids Close 26 E3
St. Florence Parade 26 H3
St. Georges Street 26 G4
St. Johns Hill 26 G3
St. Julians Street 26 H3
St. Julians Terrace 26 H3
St. Marys Street 26 G4
St. Nicholas Cres. (Penally) ..26 H5
Station Road 26 G4
Strawberry Gardens (Pen.) .26 H6
Strawberry Lane (Penally) .26 H6
Sutton Street 26 G4
Trafalgar Road 26 G4
Tudor Square 26 H3
Tudor Way 26 E3
Upper Frog Street 26 G3
Upper Hill Park 26 F2
Upper Park Road 26 G3
Victoria Cottages 26 G4
Victoria Street 26 G4
Wallsfield 26 G3
Warren Street 26 G3
Waterwynch Lane 26 G1
Weston Terrace 26 G3
White Lion Street 26 G3
Zion Gardens 26 G3

TREGARON
Population: 870
Market Day: Tuesday

Bryn Heulog 37 D1
Chapel Street 37 C2
Dewi Road 37 C3
Gardens View 37 D2
Glangro 37 D2
Glanllyn 37 D2
Heol Pontrhydpendigaid ...37 D2
Heol y Mynydd 37 D2
High Street 37 D2
Lampeter Road 37 C3
Llys Einon 37 D1
Lon Caron 37 D1
Lon y Ficerdy 37 D1
Lon yr Ystrad Maesamlwg ..37 C2
Maesamlwg 37 D2
Maesyrawel 37 D2
Parc Modur 37 C2
Penrodyn 37 C2
Rhydfawnog 37 D2
Rose Terrace 37 C2
Square, The 37 D2
Station Road 37 D1
Well Street 37 D2
Ystrad yr Orsaf 37 D1

TUMBLE Y TYMBL
Population: 2840

Banc y Gors 34 G6
Bethania Road 34 G5-H4
Bethesda Road 34 E5-F4
Darren Las 34 G6
Derwen Road 34 E4
Gors Road 34 G6
Gwendraeth Road 34 E4
Heol Bryngwili 34 H4
Heol Hirwaun Olau 34 F4
Heol y Bryn 34 G5
Heol y Neuadd 34 F4
High Street 34 F5
Kew Gardens 34 H5
Llannon Road 34 G6
Llechyfedach 34 H4
Llety Road 34 G6
Maesgwern 34 E4
Penparc 34 F5
Railway Place 34 F5
Railway Terrace 34 E4
Rhosnewydd 34 E4
Singleton Road 34 E4
Station View 34 E4
Tir Beca 34 F5
Troedy Bryn 34 F5
Tyisha Road 34 F5

WHITLAND HENDY-GWYN
Population: 1470
Market Day: Friday

Bryngwenllian 35 C2
Cross Street 35 B2
Dairy Cottages 35 B2
Gladstor Terrace 35 B3
Glendale Terrace 35 B3
Intermediate Terrace 35 B2
King Edward Street 35 B2
Lon Hywel 35 A1
Market Street 35 B2
Millbrook 35 B2
Millfield 35 B2
North Road 35 B2
Rose Cottages 35 D1
Spring Gardens 35 C2
St. Johns Street 35 B2
St. Mary Street 35 B2
Station Road 35 B2
Velfrey Road 35 A1
West Street 35 A1